THE TRUTH ABOUT FAILURE

DAVID ADAM KURZ

CONTENTS

DEDICATION

This book is for the relentless entrepreneurs who rise each day and confront challenges on their ascent to the pinnacle. To you, the visionary; eager to share your insight, invention, or message with the world. To those still hesitating to breathe life into their dreams, may this book be the nudge you need. To the resilient souls who've weathered setbacks on the path to success — without those trials, you wouldn't be where you are, nor set on becoming who you aspire to be tomorrow. Embrace it. It's your journey.

And to the critics, the skeptics, and the keyboard warriors quick to judge: may this book shift your perspective towards a path illuminated by understanding and connection.

This is dedicated to you.

The Marine Corps motto is *Semper Fidelis*.
Latin for "Always Faithful."
Imagine if the Marine Corps motto was
"Fail Forward."
How safe would you feel?

David Adam Kurz
Sergeant
United States Marine Corp 1995-2004

PREFACE

David is not only a great entrepreneur and tremendous leader in the real estate world, he is also a fantastic father, friend, and man of honor. I've truly enjoyed every interaction with him since the moment I met him, whether it be business or personal. If David is speaking it, advising it, or writing it, we should all be listening to it.

— NICK SARNICOLA FOUNDER, CATALYST
GROUP WWW.SOLARWITHFREEDOM.COM

If you are looking for truth with a little more truth sprinkled on top, then this book is a MUST READ! In a world overflowing with "talking heads" and "gurus" who have no track record of success for themselves (but somehow have a MILLION YouTube followers) entrepreneurs need to learn from individuals like David.

David is a Big Thinker and a Big Doer. David has trained, coached and mentored MANY! I myself was a client of David Kurz a few years back, and today, my Independent, Minority Owned, Real Estate Brokerage is ranked #188 in the Inc 5000! David helped me see things I couldn't see and he helped me build a blueprint that would eventually help me realize MY DREAMS AND GOALS! I'm 100% confident that you will learn and grow after reading this book.

— JEFF GARZA FOUNDER, RED BIRD REALTY
WWW.REDBIRD-REALTY.COM

My experiences over the last decade with David Kurz have been nothing short of astounding. Having our relationship blossom from colleagues to friends have made a profound impact in my life both professionally and personally. He is family. The road together has and always will bring obstacles our way and it's refreshing to know you can overcome them with someone like him by your side. I have always and will continue to wish upon many blessings to my dear friend and his journey. I'm very much looking forward to our speaking endeavors together as well as our overall growth as men!

— RUDY HERNANDEZ FOUNDER, NU WORLD TITLE LLC CO-AUTHOR, THE BLUEPRINT WWW.NUWORLDTITLE.COM

Over the years, I've had the privilege of working closely with David on incredible events and initiatives, and it's been an inspiring journey to witness his multifaceted talents and unwavering dedication.

David is a true visionary who possesses the unique ability to turn dreams into reality. His new book, The Truth About Failure, is a testament to his expertise and passion for helping others achieve their goals and reach new heights in life and business.

David's coaching programs have empowered countless individuals to overcome obstacles, set and achieve ambitious goals, and develop the mindset needed for success. His guidance is not only practical but also deeply motivating, making him a transformative force in the lives of many.

As a successful businessman, David has demonstrated exceptional leadership and strategic thinking. His ability to navigate the complexities of the business world and consistently achieve impressive results is a testament to his acumen and determination. He is a role model for aspiring entrepreneurs and business leaders everywhere.

Whether on stage or in intimate settings, David's words have the power to inspire and ignite a fire within his audience. His passion for personal development and self-improvement is contagious, and he has the rare ability to connect with people on a profound level.

Collaborating with David has been an absolute pleasure. His professionalism, enthusiasm, and commitment to excellence have made every endeavor a resounding success. He leads by example and has a natural ability to bring out the best in those around him.

The Truth About Failure is a valuable resource for anyone seeking to achieve their dreams and unlock their full potential. It has been an honor to work alongside David, and I look forward to witnessing his continued success and the positive impact he will undoubtedly have on countless lives.

— PAVAN AGARWAL FOUNDER OF
CELLIGENCE INTERNATIONAL CREATOR

OF ANGEL AI CEO SUN WEST MORTGAGE COMPANY WWW.ANGELAI.COM

David Adam Kurz, a remarkable author, speaker, and entrepreneur, has left an indelible mark on the world of motivational literature with his groundbreaking book, "Truth About Failure." The profound insights and actionable guidance encapsulated in this tome are a testament to Kurz's unique grasp on human potential and resilience. Having had the privilege of being his coaching client, I can personally attest to the transformative impact of his methods. His innate ability to connect, inspire, and elevate individuals through his speaking and coaching is truly unparalleled. "Truth About Failure" is not just a book; it's a testament to David's lifelong dedication to empowering individuals to turn challenges into stepping stones. I wholeheartedly recommend David Adam Kurz to anyone seeking to redefine success and embrace the journey of self-discovery.

I am the owner of Oceans Luxury Realty. I have had the honor of knowing David as a great friend, business coach and a phenomenal business owner, with years of extensive experience. I highly recommended David and this amazing book.

— CRYSTAL ANDERSON OWNER, OCEANS
LUXURY REALTY
WWW.OCEANSLUXURYREALTY.COM

INTRODUCTION

I'm a big believer that each person is responsible for his or her success. That's not to say they have to do everything by themselves. It's more to say that it's up to each individual to find the tools, resources, cultivate the talent, partner wisely, put in the time, and find the right mentors to live a healthy, happy, and wealthy life. To that end, I genuinely love what I do.

"What do you do?" - is a loaded question. As humans, we do it all. I work, I cook, I exercise, I love riding my motorcycle, I travel, etc. I am a mixture of how I spend my time and the thoughts that initiate my words and provoke me to action. But for the sake of introducing myself and this book to you, I'll answer what I do, as in, for a living.

I love to coach business owners and entrepreneurs. I started doing it before I knew I was doing it. It started with offering pieces of advice to people asking me for advice, to people willing to pay for my advice! At first, I was only coaching in the real estate industry, but over the years, I've realized that every business has similar struggles and the path to success, though different for everyone, has identical systems and processes that bring people success. Now, I'm the proud founder and senior coach of The Freedom Organization – a coaching service for those serious about success in all areas of life.

I also love that I get asked to speak at events nationwide. One of the best feelings is to go somewhere new, get introduced, and as I'm walking on the stage, I hear someone yell out, "Oorah!" That, of course, is the Marine Corps way to say, "Hell Ya!" That indicates to me that the person saw and heard me speak somewhere and that he or she remembered me. Even better is when someone who saw me speak years before tells me that my words helped change their lives. It's humbling and invigorating at the same time.

I also work in real estate and I love it. I love helping first-time homebuyers find their forever home. I love helping veterans who would have sacrificed everything for this great country secure a piece of the land they signed up to protect and make it theirs. It's incredibly satisfying. Knowing I'm a part of good people who get so happy they burst out in tears is a special feeling. Finally, I love helping the agents on my team develop into rock stars. My team is amazing.

I believe in striving for abundance. The only way we can help anyone else is if we get selfish about getting ourselves straightened out and prosperous. Selfishness has taken a bad rap lately. The word gets misinterpreted at times. I selfishly do all these things because it makes me feel good and provides for my family. There's nothing wrong with that.

My wife and I love to travel. We've been to 25 of the great 50 states of America. The goal is to visit every National Park, fish in lakes in Texas, put my feet in the sands of California, drive through winding roads watching the foliage in the Autumn in Maine, swim in the Great Lakes of Michigan, and create many other priceless memories in this great country. In order to do that and more, I am incredibly passionate about my success, which means I am highly passionate about the success of my team and those I am humbled to serve.

Some say failure is a part of success. They coined the words "fail forward." Well, I don't believe that. As a matter of fact, I don't believe in failure. To double down on that – I would coin the phrase "F*CK FAIL-

URE"! This simple yet difficult-to-attain mentality comes from one thought. If you never give up, it is impossible to fail.

By all stats and defaults, I am supposed to be a complete failure in life. I was born and raised in the ghettos of The Bronx. My mother was a single mom. I am half Hispanic and half Jewish. I didn't meet my father until I was 29 years old. I grew up in The Bronx but was forced to move to Miami when my mother divorced my stepfather. I hated Miami and Miami hated me. I did not fit in. I skipped many classes and dropped out of high school. Every statistic would tell you that I'd live a life of crime or barely above the poverty line. Winner, right?

However, the person writing you is a nine-year USMC Veteran, serial business owner, holder of a Master's degree in International Business, with a fantastic wife and well-adjusted, happy kids (as much as teenagers can be)! Getting here was not easy, but anything of value is not supposed to be. There are many things I've learned along the way, but the biggest and most important is never to give up. Regardless of your current problems, they will disappear just as past issues have faded from your life. Sure, new ones will rise, which is why it's time to put your pants on, buckle your belt up tight, put the panic attack away, and focus on attaining your goals, come what may.

To me, success is found in freedom: financial freedom, time freedom, location freedom, freedom to be me, etc. That's my drug of choice. That's what juices me to get out of bed early, go to the gym, reach as many people as I can, be of service to them and this country, be the best husband and father I can be, and wind down with a whiskey and a cigar proud of how I've spent the day and eager to do it again tomorrow.

I can't say how many people I've helped, but it's a lot. The truth is, I'm just getting started. But that's enough about me. I didn't write this book for me; I wrote it for you – the dreamer, the goal setter, the person who was courageous enough to start a business, the business owner who has lost passion and zeal for the baby they created and once loved. This book is for business professionals at every level. I have experiences and resources that can help you take your business and life to the next level.

The main problem I've found is that accepting failure as a necessary stepping-stone to success has become acceptable. Don't buy it, that's bullshit.

I hope this book becomes a lifetime guide. I have gathered much-needed information, stories, anecdotes, and personal experiences that should allow anyone to bring it back from the shelf and re-read it when they are at a crossroads. This book may come to you when you're at the peak of your professional career or the depths of despair, worrying if you're going to close your business or if you have three offices and your team is content but you feel you need to open a fourth. Allow this book to be a guide that navigates you around the pitfalls of failure.

My company's motto is to impact the lives and businesses of a million people. I hope this book does just that. That it reaches the single father no one cares about solely because he's a man, the single mother raising kids on her own while juggling a career, the married couple on the verge of divorce because the business has been a burden and they are stressed over finances, and everyone in between.

Ultimately, I hope it finds you when you need it. I hope you come back to it when no one is buying, when you're not getting enough business, when your staff is unhappy and not providing the support they used to, when someone is threatening to sue you, or when life is great, but you want more.

I want to stress that you are not alone. You are a courageous entrepreneur who has risked everything in your entrepreneurial journey. Focus on success, not on failing to figure things out and doing it better the next time. Never give up on yourself and your dreams. Never give in. Never let anyone or any statistic control or limit you. You are a winner. You are amazing. You are beautiful. You are more than capable of living the life you desire.

Remember, if you never give up – you can never fail.

GET YOUR FISH

FAIL FORWARD?

I'm a big believer that America, with all her problems and trials, is still the land of opportunity. However, I worry for her. Let me explain why...

Generations ago, people from all walks of life came with not much but the shirts on their backs to live a life free of tyranny. Through many struggles, as generations went on, they built the most powerful nation on the planet in just a little more than a couple of hundred years. But have you talked to a teenager lately? Where has our work ethic gone that formed this country? Forget the teenagers, how about the 20 and 30-year-olds? How about those who are addicted to 10-second Tik Tok videos and Reels? (And I'm talking about everyone with a cell phone, from kids to 75-year-olds!) How did we, as a nation, get so *soft*?

I'll tell you why.

We've gotten weak and soft because somehow, someway, we've adopted the mentality that it's okay to accept failure.

I got something to say about that. F*ck Failure!

1

There's a saying I resonate with – Fortune Favors the Bold. In other words, you can get what you want out of life, but you have to have the determination to get it. I read a story about Elon Musk, the richest man in the world. He still works 100 hours a week. He still gets so tired that he, the billionaire, sleeps on the couch in his office at times. This is the same guy that thought starting a car company wasn't worth it unless it could have a global impact, so he started an electric car company. He then had a goal to create spaceships. He did. Now he's saying he's going to colonize Mars. I believe him.

Why? Because he's not afraid to fail. He doesn't envision himself failing; he sees and focuses on his goals. People like that can live the lives they design for themselves and change their world in the process. I wrote this book to share something you need to know; you can too!

There's another saying that has gotten popular in entrepreneurial circles the last few years. That saying is, *Fail Forward*. Have you heard that nonsense? That saying literally permits people to fail. Motivational gurus and so-called coaches are giving people permission to fail! As a result, far too many people believe that failure is a necessary part of success. Well, I don't believe this and neither should you. The only way you can fail is if you quit. If you're still in the game, even though you may be losing or not where you'd like to be, it's not a failure. You have another run in you, a second wind, - a new technique that can change the game for you!

Forbes states that 87% of businesses crash and burn in the first five years. Good, intelligent, hard-working people are failing over and over again. However, since they feel they're failing forward, they think they're where they need to be in order to get to their desired destination.

Do you think the United States of America would have the most dominant military in the world if the brave immigrants that trekked here from different parts of the world accepted that failure is part of the growing process? As you read this book, I'll share with you stories of my life, but first, let me state that I'm a proud veteran of the US Marine Corps. Our motto is (The Marine Corps' motto), Semper Fidelis – "Always Faithful." That simple phrase encapsulates our eternal and collective commitment to the SUCCESS (not failure) of our battles, the progress of our nation, and the steadfast loyalty to the fellow Marines we fight alongside.

Can you imagine if we changed our motto to, "Fail Forward?" Do you think the Marine Corps would still be the most elite fighting force on the planet?

If, when in boot camp, they taught recruits that it's okay to fail so long as they fail forward from the beginning, the United States of America would soon cease to exist.

During WWII, brave men of this country dutifully answered the call to fight halfway across the world. The strong women who stayed had to stop being "just housewives" and joined the workforce, working in assembly lines and other jobs that were once only for men. These amazing women even took over major league baseball to ensure America's pastime did not slip away. Imagine if the men of that era believed failure was acceptable because we'd learn from it and didn't join the fight? Imagine if the women thought it'd be a good lesson for their husbands and sons to fail, so they didn't go to work? I'll tell you what would have happened; the economy would have collapsed, and the result would have been disastrous for the United States of America.

Why, then, do people think failing is okay? It's not!

YOU ARE NOT ENTITLED TO SUCCESS

Let me say that I'm rooting for your success; however you define it, I hope you find it. But let me also say you're not entitled to it. No one is.

Elon Musk and many other wildly successful people didn't get their fortunes handed to them. They fought for them; they cried for them, they bled for them. I saw a video clip of Bishop TD Jakes, in it, he says, "I have never met anybody who became incredibly successful in any area of their life until they have suffered and sweated and sacrificed, but kept their focus and fought through the tears and trials and tests. If you have a dream, and you commit to it, it will come to pass!"

Success is not an entitlement.

In fact, in most cases, growing up in a very successful environment is a detriment, not a right of passage.

There's a saying that goes:

Hard times create strong men.

Strong men create good times.

Good times create weak men.

Weak men create hard times.

The transference of wealth in generations is summed up like this:

My grandfather walked ten miles to get to work every day.

My father walked five miles to go to work every day.

I drive a Cadillac to go to work every day.

My son will be driven by his driver in a Rolls Royce to work every day.

His son will walk ten miles to get to work every day.

You who are reading this right here, right now, believe me when I tell you - I want you to be successful. To do that you have to do three things:

1. Never quit
2. TAKE ACTION
3. Learn to say, Failure is not an option.

Before you misinterpret me, let me clarify something – I don't have my head in the clouds and think that life is always sunshine and rainbows. Hard times are going to come for everybody. You are not going to meet your desired result all of the time. However, you have to understand this great truth - if you've never quit, you've never failed.

In business, if something isn't going your way, you have options. You can pivot. You can reassess. You can add a partner or change partners.

You can try new tactics. You can try harder. You can stay up later. You can work through the weekend. You can utilize new technology. You don't have to accept failure and quit.

IF I COULD BE LIKE MIKE

As a kid, I'd watch the NBA and then play hoops immediately after and imagine being like Michael Jordan. But as good as my imagination was, I was still a skinny half Puerto Rican, half Jewish kid from the Bronx with a decent jumper but not much hops. I mirror that to today's entrepreneurs. We see super successful business owners, so we start a business, thinking we'd be like them. We see the results but we don't see the work that was put in to achieve said results. Wishful thinking didn't work for me when I was a kid and it doesn't work for adults today.

The problem is that, in this day and age, there's an intoxicating sense of entitlement that blurs reality. It comes from having the world's knowledge at our fingertips. Suppose you want to start a digital marketing agency, coaching, or sneaker brokering business. Whatever the case, you could get all the information on YouTube or Google on how to get it started. So, people start businesses, thinking that because others are successful at it, they will be as well. They've seen a few videos on how to do it and think, how hard can it be? Ummm. Very hard.

Again, 87% of businesses don't make it more than five years!

You are not entitled to success! However, you can sure as shit work smart and hard for it. The words humble and apprentice once meant that someone was on track to future success. Today, the entitled see those words as silly or less-than, which is a great reason why they fail.

The greatness of this country was built by former generations who understood the quiet strength of humility and didn't have inflated senses of egos. People who became wildly successful sought out to find a mentor and, at times, begged to be their apprentice. It's still the best way to be successful. It sure beats striking out on your own with no experience and even less patience.

To be a doctor, you still have to undergo many years of schooling to get your doctorate degree or license. Then you have to intern (residency) for around $30K a year while being worked to the bone as you treat and align everyone that gets in front of you. During that time, you put into practice that which you learned in the classroom and things you never dreamt you'd encounter. You would do it over and over and over again, maybe sleeping on a friends sofa who lives closer to the hospital because you would be on call six nights a week. Yet, once your "apprenticeship" is over, you'd be a highly qualified doctor on the road to success.

Apprenticeship is still the best way to succeed. I am asking for your permission to allow me, during this brief time, to be your mentor as I guide you through many business pitfalls safely to your desired destination.

Before you embark on this journey with me, I'd like you to shift your mindset a bit. I'd like for you to take the word, *failure*, and replace it with the word, *hiccup*. Failure is final. A hiccup is a momentary blip. Once you've accepted failure, you're done. When you have hiccups, you can scare them away or drown them in a gallon of water.

THE LAKE

In this book are answers you've been searching for. I'm going to show you how to stop failing and how to start treating your hiccups. Should you develop the game-winning mindset I've laid out for you in this book and apply them in all areas of your life, I promise you that you will be changed for the better.

Put it this way – I have a lake, and in it are thousands of hungry fish that I've personally flown in for you. Surrounding the lake is a massive pier that goes all the way around it. The pier also stretches over it in many areas, allowing you to have access to all parts of the lake. On the pier are several fishing poles, tackle boxes, and the best bait to catch fish. In some places on the pier are ladders that you can take that lead to boats and canoes. You can literally go to any part of the lake to find the plentiful fish that swim in it. I didn't fail you.

This book is the lake. The knowledge is the fish. I can't force you to pick up a fishing pole and fish just like I can't force you to read and implement my teachings. That, my friend, you have to do for yourself. Grab a sharpie, get ready to take some notes, and get a fire started. In other words, turn the page, grab the nearest fishing pole, and get your fish!

2

BREAK OUT THE VIOLIN

TO HELL WITH STATISTICS

By all accounts, statistics, and by default, I'm supposed to be a complete and utter failure. There are many people in jail, homeless, or destitute who have a similar past as me. There are also many who have climbed higher obstacles than me, but the fact remains, if you knew my past, you wouldn't expect me to turn out the way I did.

Here are some of the things that have happened to me. I was:

- Born and raised, half Puerto Rican, half Jewish – the whitest "Rican" in the New York City hood.
- Raised by a single mother from early on.
- Met my father when I was 29 years old. I spent my entire childhood, teenage years, and 20s without him.
- My mother worked and studied and was never home.
- My stepfather only spoke Spanish and we had little in common.
- Moved from my NY home to Miami at the start of High School due to my mother and stepfather getting divorced.

- I've been beat, jumped, and fought my whole life.
- At 11, I had a severe battle with Rheumatic fever that left me weak.
- At the young age of 15, I found myself nearly paralyzed with Rheumatoid arthritis!
- I dropped out of high school.
- I lost friends to both war and stupidity.
- I suffer from PTSD from my time in the US Marine Corps.
- I divorced three times.
- I've been locked up.
- I've been backstabbed and cheated by my closest business associates.
- I've had a lot and I've lost a lot.

I know right? Break out the violin! Statistics show that most fatherless boys that grow up in the hood never leave it. Many that do bring the hood with them to wherever they go. Statistics will tell you that a Puerto Rican male from the Bronx raised by a single mother might see as much of a prison cell as they do the outside world. Statistics will tell you the trauma of not knowing your father is a gateway and excuse for acting out and defying authority. Statistics will tell you that a high school dropout is least likely to be more successful than college graduates. Statistics will tell you.... You know what? Screw the statistics.

I'm here to tell you that whatever you have gone through, whatever hell, whatever trauma, whatever was done to you – nothing and no one but you can make you successful or a failure.

FROM THE BOOGIE TO THE VICE TO THE CORPS

I grew up with zero privilege. Growing up in the Bronx was not easy. I grew up in a predominantly Puerto Rican and Dominican neighborhood. It was one of the more challenging, harder-hit economic neighborhoods in the Burroughs. What made it a little harder for me was that it looked like I didn't belong even though I was half Puerto Rican, raised by a Puerto Rican and spoke like a Puerto Rican. My biological father, whom I never knew until later in life, was Jewish, and my mother was a very fair-skinned Puerto Rican with green eyes. You can probably imagine how badly I fit in. I was the out-of-place gringo in the Spanish hood.

Thankfully, my mother was very protective of me, probably overprotective. But she did create a type of shield around me by not letting me be outside alone often. She would continually tell me I was special and to be a good example. Her guidance early on is probably the biggest reason I didn't do what most of the neighborhood kids were doing that got them in and out of jail.

She married an Ecuadorian man early in my life who helped raise me. He was an incredible guy and did his best with me. He couldn't speak English; so, we had a deal in the house, he would only talk to me in English, and I would only talk to him in Spanish; that way, we could both be better in the other language. When my brother (Manny) was born our relationship changed a bit. It became obvious that Manny was of his blood, and I was not. I don't think he intentionally meant to make me feel that way, but it happened. Then came a lot of fighting and arguing between my mother and him. Suddenly, without warning, BOOM, they divorced. I was 13 and Manny was 5. Shortly after, my mother moved us from the Bronx to Miami – or as I used to say back in the day, from the Boogie Down Bronx to Miami Vice.

I had just started getting my groove in the Bronx. I had done so well in school that I had been selected to attend a special academy, but suddenly, there I was with my Timberland boots, NY Yankees ball cap, and baggie jeans in 95-degree weather surrounded by kids with Zeke Cavarricci outfits and pointed shoes. I went from not fitting in, to fitting in, to not fitting in again.

The first time I entered my new school, I looked around and damn near had a panic attack. I was a skinny kid who had really bad arthritis (more on that later) and stuck out like a sore thumb. Right then and there, I decided to quit school.

I turned around and started to walk out, and, out of nowhere, a kid grabbed my shoulder and asked, "You from New York?" I nodded a yes. "Come on, we hang out over here."

I never realized it until now, as I'm writing this book, but I'm not sure how my life would have turned out if not for that simple, little conversation. I stayed in school and I'm glad I did. It didn't take me long to realize that my school in New York was far advanced to the one in Miami to the point that I could skip most of my classes, show up on Test Days, and pass with straight A's. However, this "superpower" alienated the phony "New York City" kids, so I ended up hanging out with a more intellectual crowd. (Honestly, it didn't bother me; most of the "NY" kids that grew up in Miami only knew hip-hop and urban attire. As my mother always said, you are who you're with. I was fine not being with wannabes.)

After 10th grade, I went to spend the summer at my stepfather's house. During that time, Hurricane Andrew tore Miami up, including the house we were renting. My mother and brother had to move into a FEMA trailer. I was getting used to Miami but had no problems staying in New York for my Junior year. I had no idea what I was in for.

I left a kid and returned to a huge school where everyone, including teachers, had to pass through metal detectors. They did that for a reason; the school I was in was known for being... violent. I got into fights—plenty of them. Sometimes I couldn't even tell my stepfather why because I legitimately didn't know. Fights just happened at that school. Things got so bad that I ended up getting jumped by a group of kids – a gang – and ended up in the hospital. My mother made me see the reality that if I stayed there, I could get killed. Sitting in a hospital room did the rest of the convincing, so I went back to Miami for my senior year.

Bored in Miami because the curriculum was too easy and I couldn't resonate with many kids there, I ended up dropping out in the 12th grade. During this time, my mother and I argued a lot. I can honestly say 99% of it was my fault. Like many other 17 and 18 year olds, I thought I had this whole life-thing figured out and nobody could tell me different. Boy, was I wrong!

One day, my mother took my car keys from me. In my anger, I stood on top of the hood of the car and punched the windshield over and over again until I smashed it, smashing my hand in the process. Ya, I had shit figured out all right.

I ended up getting kicked out of my house and moved in with my friend, Sergio. I went to night school and got my high school diploma and had a job at Wendy's. Things were beginning to look up. But something from somewhere deep inside of me told me I wasn't created to work drive-thru at a fast-food joint. It wasn't that I was unhappy so much that I felt uneasy. As if I'm not where I'm supposed to be to get me to where my life should be.

Soon thereafter, I went to Wendy's one day early for my shift. My manager, a short tiny woman who screamed more than talked, asked me to punch in early because they were busy. She didn't exactly ask; she did her best to yell in my face, which put her eyeballs right around my chin. Either way, I heard her, as did the other employees, as did the customers. As I was putting on my headset to begin my shift early, I looked around at the other employees, none of them looked happy. A scream from the manager brought my attention to her as she yelled at one of the cooks. I thought in my head that he shouldn't take that sort of abuse. Then I realized that I had just taken that abuse.

I had a moment of clarity. *This is not the life I want for myself.*

I put down my headset and walked out and never returned.

About thirty minutes later, Sergio and I were walking the mall. We weren't shopping because we didn't have any money. I just wanted to walk and clear my head after quitting. As we were walking, two men caught my attention. I looked at one and he looked directly back at me. Once they passed us, I asked Sergio who they were.

"Oh, they're Marines, the baddest military force on the planet, bro."

I stopped and turned around and the guy who I had locked eyes with was facing me, with his arms folded across his chest. "You want to talk to me, don't you?"

"Hell ya, I do."

I went to his office and immediately started the process to join. I wished they could have taken me that very day because after that conversation, I was back at the house with Sergio, broke as a joke with no food and hunger to spare.

We created a half-assed plan to go to the supermarket and steal some food. There were three of us, enough for one to steal the meat, one to steal the beans, and one to steal the cheese in order to eat some chili. I ended up getting caught, the other two got away. They got beans and chili that night and I earned the nickname the Hamburglar. I called my mother to bail me out, but she had warned me that if I got myself in jail, she wouldn't help me – and true to her word, she didn't.

That one idiotic decision put me at risk of joining the Marine Corps. I had to write a letter to the Corps to explain what had happened. I had never been so embarrassed. I realized that even though I didn't come from much, I had a lot of pride. Had I not, I would have called my mother and told her I was hungry instead of becoming the Hamburglar. My recruiter vouched for me and I was allowed to join.

The night before going to Boot Camp, I soaked my wrist in water, took a pair of scissors, and cut off the cast on my wrist from punching the windshield. The following morning, I left with a fractured hand to match my fractured pride. Little did I know, life was about to throw a lot more at me than I ever thought I'd be able to handle.

CLARITY AND INSANITY

Some people think that a moment of clarity is when the clouds part and everything they need to do in life appears in front of them. Maybe that's how it is for some, but not me. On the day I left Wendy's, I had a moment of clarity. Hell, I had no idea what I wanted out of life at the time but I knew I wasn't on the road for whatever it was. I just knew I was not where I was meant to be at that moment in time and if I didn't make a change, I'd never get there.

Maybe, you're not where you need to be. Maybe not in your career, relationship status, or geographic location. Examine your life as it is right now. I'm not asking you to look into your future and create a vision board, I'm asking you to look at where your feet are at this very moment. Are you where you need to be? I'm not asking if you're where you are destined to be. That's a different question.

Before one can change course or pivot in their lives, one first needs to assess where they are. Be attentive. What opportunities have you let slip by? I want you to realize that your best thinking got you exactly where you are, so if you don't like where you are, it's your thinking that got you there. Who do you know that you should ask to mentor you? Who should you take out to lunch to figure out how they've gotten so successful in marriage, as a parent, or in business?

A moment of clarity is closely related to a moment of insanity. At times, deciding who you will be during your moment of clarity can get you to do crazy things.

But that's okay. I have interviewed many incredibly successful and wealthy people in the last five years, and many of them have told me that it was the moments of what others would call insanity that got them to a higher level.

I left a job on bad terms – that manager was not going to give me a good reference. I was too proud to ask my own mother for food, which made me hungry enough to steal. I was on a slippery slope leading to disastrous results. I didn't know what I wanted out of life. But when I saw those Marines turn the corner, even though it made no sense, even though I had no idea what I was getting myself into, I knew I was meant for more.

Are you meant for more? I want you to start becoming aware of the opportunities that are going to present themselves to you. The word, Luck, is sometimes defined as – preparedness meeting opportunity. Well, if you're not preparing to meet opportunity, you're going to be shit out of luck. Your mindset shift begins with when you believe you were put on this planet for a great purpose.

Oh, and screw the statistics. Just because some of the people I grew up around became junkies or career criminals had no bearing on what I did in my life or what some of my other friends that found their way out did. I've known sons of alcoholics that don't drink alcohol and sons of non-drinkers that become alcoholics. I know people who got out of jail and went back in and some that got out of jail and became highly productive members of society. I hate when I'm watching a sports show and they talk about the history of a team - what happened ten years ago has no bearings on the players in today's game. Most statistics are bullshit. You don't have to stay where you came from and you don't have to be the person people expect you to be. Know this, you and only you are in control of your future. Create your own stat.

3

IT'S ABOUT TIME

TIME

If someone tells you there is only one way to be successful – they're trying to sell you something. Many roads lead to success. It doesn't matter if you are married, single, fat, skinny, white, black, brown, Christian, Buddhist, Atheist, Jewish, male, female, a drinker, or sober; they have all been successful and have all done it differently. However, most successful people have a few things in common, and this is one of them – they are willing to work hard to achieve what they want, desire, and demand out of life!

The single biggest thing you need to sacrifice on the road to success is your time. This is why you need to stay motivated. I like to watch motivational videos, listen to business shows, and network, network, network. You'll notice that I reference Elon Musk often, that's out of the respect I have for him. He was the first billionaire who said he would build a spaceship. At first, he was mocked and ridiculed, but still, he did it. Now, Jeff Bezos and others are trying to do the same thing. If you're under forty at the time of this writing, I believe, and it's wild that I'm writing this, that you will witness people leave Earth to colonize Mars, thanks to Elon Musk.

He was asked if he would recommend a young entrepreneur to do what he is doing. His answer was perfect, albeit totally unexpected. He said, and I'm paraphrasing,

"Don't do this. It's crazy. It hurts. It's painful. It's not a viable way to live. Don't chase entrepreneurship."

I thought that's the best advice I'd ever heard for that question.

I say it's great advice because if it deters anyone, they would have failed anyway. They would have lost money, time, and maybe even self-respect. On the other hand, if you were a true entrepreneur, it would motivate you. You would have known what you were getting into with your eyes wide open and clear expectations that it wouldn't be easy. That you would go through pains, and struggles, cry yourself to sleep, and be nervous nearly all the time, but that it would be worth it. You'd be excited to face the world with your chin up and chest out as you follow your dreams and accomplish your goals.

What you have to know about people like Elon Musk is that he's not trying to be a role model. He's not trying to fill stages. He's not selling courses. He's not running for office. He's trying to change the world. I'm not suggesting that you go out and try to change The World; I'm challenging you to go out and change Your World. If you do that, you could change the world for the people closest to you.

You have enough time in the day to create the life you want. I own multiple businesses, have a show, travel to speak, spend dinners with my family, and do many other things. As I am writing this, my 3rd book, I am also scripting a reality show, planning a two-state tour, and focusing on what my companies need to do to close out the year stronger than ever. People often ask me where I find the time. If you're worried about time, you're worrying about the wrong thing. I don't think about finding time; I'm too busy doing what needs to be done. If Elon can make electric cars and spaceships in the same 24 hours I have, I can do what I have to do too!

I hate when people use time as an excuse for not doing something. It's such a weak cop-out.

Time is not their problem. Prioritizing is their problem, but they won't take personal responsibility for their actions so they blame it on the lack of time.

When you get up in the morning, do what you do – meditate, pray, go to the gym – all of that is good. Get your morning routine done that sets you up for the rest of the day because then you have the whole rest of the day!

I often have dinner with my family, especially if I'm not out of town. It's not always a sit-down dinner; sometimes, it's a makeshift dinner as we walk and talk, but it's still family time.

TELL TIME WHAT TO DO

You can either be a victim to time, not having enough of it, it can go by too fast, or you can control time. This might sound weird but I make sure not to be governed by time. I don't let time tell me what to do. I tell time what to do. I tell time that at 2 p.m. I'm meeting Rick. At 4 p.m., I'm meeting with Rudy, and at 5 p.m. I'm doing a Zoom meeting with Eli. When the appropriate time comes, I do what I told it I would do.

If you're having an issue with not having enough time in the day, do these two things.

- Make a list of priorities.
- Put everything important on your calendar – and make sure you don't put something unimportant ahead of your priorities.
- Stick to the schedule on your calendar.

I live off of my Google calendar. If something is not there, it is because it isn't important enough for me to schedule it; it may as well not exist. I block off times that are important to me. My main goal is to have freedom. To do that, I must succeed in business. My desire for freedom is to do things with and for my family. So, I put meetings, calls, events, speaking gigs, networking outings, and business opportunities on my calendar. I also put family time there: dinners with the family, outings, movie nights, etc. I also put my me-time on it; gym, meditation and prayer, hanging out with the boys.

I also use Calendly so that people can meet with me on their time. Of course, I still control the open spots on my Calendly. If you take control of your time, you'd be surprised at the abundance of time God gave you in a day.

I don't know if you're like me, but when my time on Earth is over, I don't want to be summed up in 3 words – husband, father, entrepreneur. I can't imagine living an entire life and the summary of my existence could be said in a half sentence. That's not the legacy I want to leave. By being in control of my time, I not only get done what I need to, but I do what I like to do, meaning, I'm not waiting to reach my goal to be happy, I do the things and spend time with the people that make me happy now.

The biggest difference between achievers and those who never excel is that they leverage time to get to where they want to go.

Tell time what to do and you'll be on the fast lane to success in every aspect of your life.

MY ROAD

Some business owners grew up with the entrepreneurial spirit in their bellies. Many entrepreneurs grew up selling baseball cards, candy, or whatever they could that someone would buy. They valued and went after money from an early age. I had a friend who would put his new comic books into plastic bags to keep them pristine-looking, knowing they would be much more valuable one day. That wasn't me. I was more like, just read the book, bro and let me use it when you're done! When I was a kid, I was busy being a kid.

I never thought of starting a business. I worked at Wendy's till the day I quit and joined the Marine Corps. I was halfway around the world when I got my first taste of entrepreneurship.

I was a Marine Corps corporal stationed in Iwakuni, Japan. On paper, my Staff Sergeant was in charge of the armory. In reality, I was. She had undergone a difficult surgery and helped when she could via phone or when I would swing by to see her. Seeing how businesses worked from behind the scenes was far more interesting than I ever expected. I thought it was so cool that I, who had no business experience, managed a small enterprise of a much larger entity, The United States Marine Corps.

One evening, I was walking around Hiroshima with two other Marines. We were bored and didn't know what Hiroshima offered. Ahead of us, the door of a small nightclub opened. I couldn't believe my ears. All the way in Hiroshima, Japan, I heard Merengue music! (That's very traditional Spanish music). I told my friends that it was Spanish music – they didn't know, to them (one a Caucasian from the South and the other a black man from Jamaica) it was foreign music. I convinced them to go in there and I got the second big shock of the evening. The place was full of Brazilians!

I was shocked because Brazil and Japan are not neighbors. However, their countries are very friendly with one another. Little known fact - if a Japanese citizen has a child in Brazil, that child would automatically get dual citizenship. This is known as the Japanese Nationality Law or the 1950 Nationality. As a result, many Brazilians started working in Japan and, as evidenced by the packed nightclub, they also brought their culture.

We had a blast. I continued to go there and became good friends with the owner and his sister. One day, I had an Epiphany.

"Paulo, if you just added English music, you'd get the entire base here AND the Japanese nationals."

"You think so?"

"Yeah man, everyone is bored going to the same spots and there aren't many places that play English music mixed with Spanish Music. Can you think of one? I can't. If you do it, I'll promote the hell out of it from inside the base!"

Paulo asked me if I wanted to go into business with him. I wasn't expecting that. I was just trying to help him grow his business and have fun in the process. However, I was intrigued and we went into business together.

We scouted a place called Chinatown. It was a huge space that was usually rented out for weddings and occasions, but it was built just like a nightclub. It had a VIP section, tables, bars, a DJ Booth, lighting – everything we needed. We rented it for one night to see if it would work out. I then got a part-time job at a print shop to get a discount on the flyers. I printed out 1,000 flyers – 500 in Japanese and 500 in English, which I passed out to everyone I could at the base. We worked very hard to convert Chinatown into a nightclub. Finally, the big day came.

The deal was, I would handle the door and he would handle the bar. My money would come from the door from where I would pay my staff, and his money would come from the bar and he'd pay his staff.

By 11 p.m. that first night, it was empty. A total flop! We had spent so much time and energy on it. I was embarrassed. I dreaded having to tell the people at the base that no one showed up after bragging about how amazing it would be. One of the bouncers, a Marine I hired, said he needed help finding the place, so he went out to see if others could not find the place. Almost an hour later, we had around 300 people. More than 1,000 people paid and partied at our club that night. Every two weeks, I would make about $15K-$20K. After our New Year party, after paying everyone out, I walked away with $60K. I even had a tradition with all the Marines I hired to go to breakfast Sunday mornings after the club closed, on me. The bug bit me hard. I loved being an entrepreneur!

One evening, a bouncer told me that a guy flashed his badge and wanted to come in. I greeted him and brought him in, free of charge – we weren't hiding anything. I knew he was from NCIS – Naval Criminal Investigative Services, they're like the Detectives for the Marines and Navy. He asked if I employed Marines. I proudly said, "Hell yes, they love the extra money." The Company's First Sergeant invited me to his office a few days later. This is not a typical invitation you would get as a Corporal in the Marine Corps, so I knew something was up. I was shut down immediately. It turned out that a regulation stated Marines were not allowed to work anywhere off base where alcohol was served. Everything came to a screeching halt. I had to break the bad news to my partners and they were not happy. They tried to keep it going but it wasn't successful without my team and my influence from inside the base.

I had never made money like that in my life. However, I didn't fall in love with entrepreneurship just because of the money. I loved the status it gave me, the popularity, and most importantly, the validation that I could run a thriving business.

I considered staying in Japan and running the nightclub with my partner full-time. Fate had other plans. I didn't stay there and become the Club Kingpin of Japan. Instead, I came home from Japan with a burning desire to own a business.

SHORTEN TIME

If you're reading this, it is your time.

To do what? Only you can answer that. But you just read a great way to live an extraordinary life by prioritizing the things most important to you and by telling time what to do.

You may have already started a business, if so, great! Congratulations! But now it's time to grow it. You may not have yet to start a business but are considering it. Great! It's time to get out there. Just like my experience in Japan prepared me to run a business, you also have experiences that will come into play when you start yours.

Regardless of what stage you are in business-wise, you have an advantage that I didn't. Coaching is available everywhere. Many highly qualified coaches can guide you through the murky waters of entrepreneurship.

You can shorten the time frame to reach your goal by hiring the right coach.

Understand that the best athletes, the best movie stars, and the best singers all have coaches. Guard your time, stick to your schedule, hire someone to help you get to where you want to go faster and live the life of your dreams now, and later.

TIME VALUEMENT

I attended a private, invite-only mastermind session at a friend's residence. I had the privilege of gaining deeper insights from the people in the room, who are no strangers to entrepreneurship. The friend who hosted us is also not a stranger to success, having sold a company he co-founded for $80M. Needless to say, he has a proven track record and a profound knowledge of team-building, business development, and the ever-important concept of time management. His name is Nick Sarnicola. More on him in the resource section of this book.

Rather than emphasizing on merely managing time, he introduced us to the concept and term - Time Valuement. I had always valued my time but had never put a name to it. My friend's core message revolved around dedicating oneself to tasks that inject actual value into the business while leveraging all other ancillary tasks. If you truly value your time, you would fill as much of it performing Money Making Activities - MMA's.

MMA's should always be checked off of your daily list of things to do.

To be more explicit, don't start doing anything else in your business until you have completed all of the MMA's you've set for yourself. Don't answer inquiry questions, send out email reminders, watch a motivational video or any other activity that would fill your time and not get to the MMA's.

The notion of, "I can't afford to hire." is a fallacy. You can afford to pay someone for 5, 15 or 20 hours a week. Here's the truth: if you plan to grow your business, you can't afford not to hire. Don't let fear or doubt creep into your mindset. Remember, you are a unique, creative being who believes in abundance, not scarcity. Once you hire the right person to handle supporting tasks and you get to do what you love and do best, you will realize you've already waited too long.

4

THE ROAD TO SUCCESS IS FRAUGHT WITH PERIL

FREEDOM

Here's the reality of chasing success in the form of a big car, big house, big bank account, and oversized pool; if you do what it takes to get it but have a family, your home life will likely suffer. People that want to dominate at work don't know when to quit.

You would open up a nightclub with the goal of making it for over a year because 70% of nightclubs close in their first year. After the year, you'd want to have it compete with the best clubs in the city. Then you'd like your club to be named the best in the city. Then, once you've figured out how to build a successful nightclub, you'll want to open up a second one in another city. And the chase for success will continue as you try to open nightclubs in every city. Then, assuming you're the best nightclub owner ever in the States, your kids would have grown, you'll have already missed priceless moments with your grandchildren, and if you're lucky, you're still married. However, instead of leaning back and enjoying all the wins, you'd start thinking about how to open your clubs in other countries. It's the natural progression of the high achiever.

I'm not saying to shy away from your definition of success; good God no, I just want you to be realistic about it. Don't expect to work 12 to 18-hour days at the office and expect to be a great spouse or parent. Don't expect abs of steel if you get too busy to go to the gym. It makes sense, doesn't it?

Again, take a moment now, and figure out what success means. For your sake, if you haven't yet, write it down. Refrain from feeling as if you're being egotistical if you want the most prominent house and the biggest boat. To quote the great William Shakespeare from a monologue he wrote delivered by the character Polonius – To thine own self be true. In modern slang, he is saying not to bullshit yourself. Own up to who you want to be. Who you are! Don't apologize for it. Bury it within your bones and have it drive everything you do to get what you want.

I'll tell you, unashamedly, what success means to me. First, let me state that it has changed multiple times throughout the years.

Some things that were essential years ago aren't as important to me today. As I continue to evolve, I believe I'll have a different version of success in ten years.

However, the barometer for measuring success will be different in ten years or less. It will be measured through how much time I have to be with the people I love and do what makes me happy instead of the number of offices I have, speaking gigs, and money in the bank. It will also be measured on how calm and content I am. (My wife laughs at the idea, saying I will never be calm! But I digress, let's continue.)

I've gone through so much the last three years. I've gone through more hiccups than most are comfortable admitting to publicly. During the storms I found myself in, I realized that I needed a coach. So, I hired someone to help me see above the waves that towered over my ship. I was amped and ready to divulge everything I was going through with my new coach, who came highly recommended by my good friend James, CEO and Founder of MAXA. I instantly realized why. She would keep me from getting into the stuff I wanted to talk about. She said, "First, I need to know your WHY."

I didn't understand why her knowing my why was so important when I had enemies at the gates! I tried to get into what was happening to me at the moment, so I came up with a quick *why*, but she didn't buy it. I tried to skirt around it, but she told me that if we didn't know my well-defined why, it would be impossible for her to coach me to where I wanted to go and who I wanted to be. It took us three coaching sessions – three weeks - for me to soul search without a filter and discover my why.

I want to make a significant amount of money in my life, the type that positively impacts future generations. I want to leverage the businesses I've created and reap from the blood, sweat, and tears so that they grow and add value to the other companies I've formed. But here's the kicker; I am willing to bust my ass to get that, but it's not for the cars, homes, or bling. I want to do all that to do what I want with my time. I want time with my family. I want to take time to travel. I want to have the time to do things that ordinary people may never be allowed to do because they're working and their bosses won't let them.

At the core of everything sat my why. I want FREEDOM.

I want the freedom of *having* to work. I want to be free of negative people. I want financial freedom. I want to empower others, I want to travel and speak on different stages, invest in my partnerships, brainstorm to develop better processes and systems, read books, study, educate myself, get certifications, and do all the shit I do – all of it is to provide me with the type of freedom I want. And I won't allow myself to settle for anything less.

I'm not writing my why so you can judge me. My why is independent of anyone's approval or validation. I wrote my why so that it may help you find yours. This is not an easy task to do.

You must figure out why you get up in the morning and do what you do daily!

Your why can be ever-changing and should be fluid at times. Age and life position may shift your why. For instance, when I was 26, my why was so I could have a Lambo and a mansion. Now, I have a wife and four daughters... my why has shifted to how I can spend more time with them.

Your why might be your family. Like that single mom, heaven on earth for you might be family dinners, baseball games, and tucking the kids to sleep. That's awesome. (Actually, anyone that doesn't want that probably needs to be examined.) I totally get the Family-First mantra. Having said that, I say this with respect to you and your family; if that is more important to you than your business or massive financial success, your business will suffer. But your family will expand in greatness. The conundrum is always, how do you support that family you care so much about ? For me, that is ensuring I can massively provide for them and give them as much of me as I can. They give me their full support and I go out daily to PUT IN THE WORK.

You can have many things you focus on, but there's only one priority. If the family is the priority, the business may not be as profitable as possible. If the company is the priority, the family unit may not be as tight as possible.

WORK-LIFE-BALANCE-BULL

Someone came up with a work-life-balance thought that caught fire. But it's bullshit. If you give 50% to each, neither will flourish to be all it can be. If you spend more time growing your business than at home, ensure you are very present when you're with your family. Otherwise, regardless of how successful you get, you could find yourself living in a beautiful house but alone.

Finding success is the ultimate challenge. That challenge becomes significantly more complex if you don't have someone who supports you. If your significant other continually bashes you and gets upset with you because of the time and energy you spend building your dream, you're with the wrong person. Please don't rush to get a divorce and blame it on me, but take time to evaluate the situation. Maybe you haven't expressed to the other person how important your goals are to you. Sit down with him or her and get them to share the vision. There's a saying that goes - If you want the villagers to help you build a boat, don't hire them; have them long for the open sea. If your spouse or significant other doesn't believe in you or the path you're taking, maybe try couple's therapy. Or, who knows, perhaps it's time to set you both free to either be alone or to find someone who can accept you for who you are today.

Surround yourself with people better than you - who encourage you - who will applaud you.

Sometimes, the solution is simpler than you think. Sometimes, the answer is to share your thoughts/ goals and the sacrifice you are willing to put into it so your partner can see the vision with you – and support you without losing love and affection towards you.

I met a high-producing agent who sold over a thousand properties yearly! As awesome as it is for him, his home life struggled because he hardly spent time with his wife and children. He was making great money but was on the road to a nasty, costly divorce. Luckily, he realized the road he and his wife were on and brought her into the business. Now, their quality time is being together working on growing the business. They now share the vision and support one another!

My wife, Jennyffer, a hustler like me, works with mortgages, helps manage our online coaching platform, and helps lead my real estate team. I'm a Real Estate broker and Business Coach. She gets all of our business. We have kids, so it allows her to work from home, but it also allows us to be in communication constantly. Since the pandemic and my transition to a brokerage, I now work out of a home office more often. We may not be walking down the beach, holding hands, drinking Mai Tai's every day, but we're always in close proximity to each other and aware of what the other is doing.

That works for many other high-level producers I know, not just us. However, as the saying goes, there's more than one way to skin a cat. On the flip side, I know other happy couples that are killing it; one kills it at work, and the other kills it at home or in a completely different industry. Finding success as an entrepreneur is difficult enough, but it's much more satisfying coming home after 16 hours of straight work and your spouse greets you with a hug and kiss, and you both speak about your day and share each other's successes. Although your days were very different, you share the same "home" goal, whatever that is to you and your partner. No dollar amount covers that type of value. As hard as finding true success may be, if you find the right partner and find the right balance, forget the money for a moment, you'll have a much more enjoyable life. The money would be the bonus!

BEWARE THE CRABS

One of the most significant hiccups you'll find on the road to success is the people around you. For the most part, they're like crabs in a bucket. Have you seen when one crab struggles and is finally able to get out of the bucket, one of the other crabs grabs it and pulls it back into the bucket? It happens. All too often, the crabs are not who you think they'd be. I'm sorry to tell you this, but that crab could be your mother, father, brother, sister, cousin, childhood friend, pastor, teacher, mentor, or anyone else. I hate to admit it, but I certainly have them in my family, so I don't roll in the same bucket anymore.

Most people who care for you are not intentionally sabotaging or limiting you. Maybe your idea is too innovative for them to grasp, and, in their attempt to protect you, they try to dissuade you, even if it means ridiculing you so that you 'wake up.'

They'll tell you it's a stupid idea or that someone else already thought of it. They'll remind you that you worked hard to get this good job and you shouldn't waste it to chase a dream. They'll ask you why you're wasting time doing that little business. They'll remind you that you got a college degree, and it wasn't in Business Administration, so what do you know about running a business? Dianna Kokoszka, a real estate leader, once said something along the lines of, "If your goals don't make people laugh at you, they aren't big enough."

You can't care what they think about your vision of success. It's not that you can't care for them or consider what they're saying; it's just that their vision is not yours, and that's okay. Now, if they continue to badger you and become pains in the ass, it's time to move on from them. You've outgrown them. It's not sad. It's not bad. It's just a part of life. If you keep hanging out with employees who bitch about their jobs, you'll miss out on conversations with business owners who are solving solutions as they make strides in their companies that you can implement into yours.

The sad truth is that you're going to lose friends. Not every business partner will treat you ethically, professionally, and kindly. People will attack you – publicly and privately. People will smile at your face and compliment you, only to walk away and tell others how fake you are or that you're delusional or a liar. Although it will feel like a personal attack, the truth is that the people that hate on you portray what they're going through to you. Your unashamed ambition makes them nervous. The fact that you will do what it takes to live the life you design for yourself makes them feel insignificant and cowardly for not going after their dreams, so they lash out.

I've had my share of disputes with so-called friends, some publicly and some privately. In my industry, I thought I had formed tight bonds with many people who would come to my home, eat with my family and me, and who I'd go out of my way for – only to have them become something different. Once, a friend called me and told me what one of my so-called friends said about me on social media. I hadn't seen it because I'm too busy building than looking for drama. He asked me, "What are you going to do about it? How are you going to respond?" I answered, "I'm not giving that guy any of my energy. I don't have time for that. I know who I am, how I conduct business, and what's important to me. Let the hater hate.

If/when jealousy rears its ugly head within your circle and you get attacked, my advice is to ignore it. It's white noise. There's no music to it, no harmony, no vibes; it's just white noise, background noise. The haters and the stupid will always be there. Keep climbing until they're so far below you, you can't see or hear them anymore.

Shedding friends is par for the course. Sure, in an ideal world, the road to success ends with you throwing a massive party with every person you ever cared about and known they're celebrating with you.

In the real world, you will lose friends. Stop worrying that your childhood best friend calls you fake or says you have changed. You're supposed to change!

I wish I could tell you that your original friends will be there when you become a multi-millionaire, but I'd be lying. The truth is, if you remain friends with people who aren't doing what you're doing, you'll never reach the level of success you want.

Have you heard the saying, "Tell me who you hang out with and I'll tell you who you are?" My mother used to say that all the time. Multi-millionaire Robert Kiyosaki, took that saying into the financial realm and said, "If you want to be rich, be friends with people who have the same mindset as you, or who at least won't try to change your mindset to be more like theirs. Life is too short to spend time with people who don't help you move forward."

So, those broke friends of yours, cut them loose. They're bringing you down. That college girlfriend of yours that still wants to party all the time, cut her loose; she's bringing you down. You don't have to be dramatic about it or even talk with them about it. That could be hurtful, and you'd gain nothing from it. Simply stop taking their calls, stop texting them all the time, don't show up and go drinking with them every Thursday, Friday and Saturday. They'll move on and you didn't burn a bridge, which is a win/win in my book.

This chapter was difficult to write without feeling negative energy. I wrote it with strong words and direction to get you thinking. I want you to start evaluating your surroundings. I cannot write a book about FAILURE and not talk to you about your surroundings. I can't let you keep trying to be successful in a bucket full of crabs. I need you to know that this is a part of the growth process and when you become vigorously attentive to it, you will fail less. You will be out of the bucket. Your bubble will pop and your circle will become smaller yet more advanced.

But stop slumping, I also have good news! The more successful you get, the more successful people you will meet. You'll start having different, solution-based conversations. You'll put yourself in a position to help those less fortunate, either in person or through a charity event. You will be able to grow with those people. And as the cycle of life continues to go full circle, you'll distance yourself from some of those friends too and find new ones.

The number of acquaintances you have increases the more successful you get, but the circle of close friends gets smaller.

Be careful who you let in your inner circle. Be selective and protective of who you allow to water your garden.

Everyone has an opinion and wants to give advice, but be picky about who you receive advice from or the direction you choose to follow.

The road to success is fraught with many dangers, even from those closest to you. Know this, they can't break you. Don't let their bullshit hold you back or take you down. The only way you fail is if you quit. Keep your eyes and attention on your prize. Allow no one to take you away from your dreams and goals.

5

AIRPORT BLUES

I want to dedicate this chapter to everyone not afraid of dreaming big dreams, putting them down on paper, and having the fortitude to take action. This is to those who won't let anyone stand in the way of what you want from life.

To you, the courageous dreamer who has sat at the airport (this part will make more sense once you've read this chapter) and figured out how much it costs to fly private, the nearest Pilot Training school to you, the time it would take to get your pilot's license, and figured out how much it costs to rent or charter a plane to get to anywhere you want to go. Amid all the stuff that has happened to you, instead of complaining about it, you haven't spent time thinking of the solution to the problem; instead, you've found the solution so that you never have that problem again. If you protect the time you've been given, your dreams will become your reality.

Oh, and I love and admire you.

I'm a planner and do everything possible to be a man of my word. If I say I will do something or be somewhere, I take personal responsibility to do it or be there. For that reason, my wife and I have TSA Clearance – TSA Pre-check, which enables us to skip the long security check line and quickly get through security without even having to take our shoes off. We also have Global Entry, which provides expedited U.S. customs screening for international travelers when entering the United States. Should we run late for a flight, for whatever reason, those measures will help us to be where we planned to be.

Recently, my wife and I made plans to attend a conference in New Jersey. Since I try to eliminate problems before they occur, we got to the airport at 11 AM for a 2:20 PM flight from Miami to Atlantic City. That was the only thing that went right at that airport.

Although I had already checked in on my phone, we had to use the check-in machines to get our tickets printed and the tags to stick on our bags. When we walked in, we saw a line of people waiting for three of the many machines that printed out the tickets. At first, I assumed that the other machines, only 100 feet away, must have failed to work since everyone was waiting on those three machines. Not being one that likes to stand around, I walked to another device and sure enough, it worked fine.

I looked at my ticket and realized it didn't have my clearances as mentioned earlier – TSA and Global Entry. We manually placed our tickets on our bags and waited forty-five minutes to drop off the bags. When it was our turn, I told the airline employee that the machine didn't print my clearances. Instead of trying to help, he said, "Ya, some-times it does, sometimes it doesn't." That was the extent of the customer service he provided. My wife and I had to wait in the long security line I'd spent time and money getting those clearances to avoid. As you can tell, I wasn't enjoying my experience with this airline. Little did I know how much worse it was about to get.

We got situated on the plane, and it got on the runway, but then, inex-plicably, it returned to the gate. There was quite a bit of rumbling after a stewardess said they needed to get mechanics to check on some instru-ments and that she appreciated our patience. Once she said she appreci-ated our patience, I knew we would be there for a while. We stayed on the plane for 3 hours. At the afore-mentioned 3 hours, they let us out of the plane to wait more comfortably in the airport waiting area.

When I got back to the airport, I quickly went to work. We would have landed in Atlantic City by the time we got back to the airport we were meant to fly out of, and I had previously scheduled two appointments and an important dinner that I had to fit in while in Jersey. I continued to do some work and catch up on things as the time ticked off the clock – and my life.

The airline gave us a $7 voucher for food, but all the restaurants were closed. Besides, the $7 wouldn't have covered a full meal had they been open. They also offered a $50 voucher for an upcoming flight, even though the $50 wouldn't cover the entire flight. The main issue was that we couldn't book another flight because we couldn't get our luggage out of the plane. In essence, we were held hostage there. My wife and I were frustrated, but everything was out of our control.

That's when I started participating in one of my favorite pastimes – People Watching. I took in the entire scene of what happened during our 8-hour wait at the airport, which is the foundation for this chapter.

PEOPLE

Many people go through reacting to things that happen to them. Because they're in a bad situation, they don't seem to have the ability or care to see how it could benefit them down the road. When you can think like that, you'll live a life thinking that things don't happen to you, they happen for you. This is what I observed:

The Victim: I saw a girl on her cellphone, crying her eyes out. She was in near hysterics, not exactly yelling but loud enough for me to hear her from across the way, "In my whole 24 years of life, I've never had to deal with this nonsense!"

My immediate thought was, *well, hold on to your horse's girl; you're only 24, and you have a whole lot more life yet to go. If you think this is as bad as things can get, you're unprepared for all life throws at you. Put your tears and hysteria away, and woman the heck up!*

The Complainer: Some people kept going to the counter to harass the employee about their situation. They would go there, ask stupid questions, get unsatisfactory answers, look around at others as if they won a point in a court case, show everyone how upset they were and stomp off and sit down, only to be in her face fifteen minutes later.

I thought, "*What do you think she's going to say differently to the same questions? You don't have to like what's happening, but at least accept the reality that in this particular time, we're stuck here. She's not a genie who can magically send you to Atlantic City, and she's not trained to fix the plane. Feeling the need to belittle someone because you're not happy is bullying and shows how much of a weak character you are.*

The Demander: Then there was that guy who felt he had all the answers. When one of the complainers sat down to think of another thing to complain about, the Know-It-All Demander shouted from his seat, "Just get us another plane! It's that simple!" And then he'd yell out stuff like, "Let's get the plane going. What's so hard about that?" It got so bad an employee called the police, most likely to ensure violence wouldn't erupt.

My thought was, *Don't you think if they had another plane, we would be on it by now? They're working on the issue. What the heck do you think they're doing, playing tiddlywinks? Yelling from your chair like a 7th-century English King isn't going to get everyone within earshot to cower and submit to you. If he acted like that in public, I would hate to see how he treated his family in the privacy of their home.*

The Spectator: Those who probably wanted to yell but didn't want to look like the fools the others showed themselves to be. However, they would nod in agreement with The Victim, The Complainer, and The Demander and encourage them to continue to harass the employee who had nothing to do with our situation.

My thought was: *Maybe if you stop giving these folks so much attention and affirmation, they'll settle down. Your apparent backing of their poor behaviors empowers them to continue. Stop paying them so much attention! Bad behavior loves attention from ignorant people.*

The Chill: That's the group my wife and I were in. We just chilled and waited. Many of us got on our laptops or phones and worked or watched Netflix or went and got a drink. We were undoubtedly frustrated but realized it was out of our control, so we made good use of the time.

My thoughts on me: *OK. I can't do anything about this. I'm forced to lose time in Atlantic City, but I am not forced to lose time. There are some things I haven't been able to get to and some things that I can get ahead of, so focus on those things.*

My dreams don't allow me to spend 8 hours being upset and unproductive.

I envision the future me, the person I strive to be, screaming at me from the future, demanding that I focus on what I can control to make that future me the present-day me. I made friends, rescheduled my appointments, and even found a way to have a few laughs.

But then a thought came to mind: I had done what I could previous to this flight to not be in this situation, and I couldn't get another flight, so I have to ride this out. But what can I do to never put myself in this situation again? Most people's solution to a problem like the one I was in is never to fly that airline again. The truth is, every airline has delays, so whether you're paying a low fare on Spirit or spending big bucks flying First Class on Qatar Airways, there's always a chance you'll encounter delays. I challenged myself to come up with a solution.

I leaned over and said to my wife, "I don't ever want to be in a situation like this ever again."

She answered, "Do you want to drive yourself everywhere?"

"Not that either, Babe. We'll get to the point where we have a private jet!"

THE BEST SOLUTIONS

The best way to avoid some problems is to ensure you don't put yourself in a position to be in them. Don't just find the solution to the problem; create solutions that prevent those problems from ever occurring.

I started to think about how much a charter plane costs. How long would it take to get a small, 6-seat plane to New Jersey, counting the few gas stops along the way? I looked it up; it's costly. Part of that cost is hiring the pilot. So then I started to look at the nearest pilot training school near me and how much time it would take and how long it would take to get a pilot's license. My thought was for me to never be in this position again, I need to have X amount of money I can put into chartering a plane and X amount of time and money to get a pilot's license.

Some people might read this and think that I think too big. Maybe I do. But other people think even bigger.

Grant Cardone bought his own plane. When asked why he bought his plane, he says that with that purchase, he also bought himself back his time. If he had a trip to New Jersey, he could have gotten on his plane and landed in Jersey at 11 AM, done what he had to do, and been back for dinner with his family. Heck, he could have taken his family to Jersey with him if he wanted.

To paraphrase, Grant Cardone didn't buy a jet; he bought time. Even though everyone would say that time is the most important thing, most people give it lip service. They don't protect their time, they don't value it, they give it away to people that abuse it or don't appreciate it.

Any airline can put you in the same situation I was in but can't force you to waste time. I was frustrated. I felt taken advantage of. I had to break my plans. I could have told a few people off, like the customer service person at the baggage drop-off who wouldn't do anything to help me and get me through the security lines as I deserved, or yelled at The Demander to calm down. I could have been so frustrated I could have started an argument with my wife and others around me. But I didn't have time for that.

You have to see beyond the bull in front of you.

You may have heard this before, but it's absolutely true – your current circumstance is not your final destination. Wherever you find yourself in your life, know this – it's a launching point to who you will be. Don't spend your time feeding off negative energy and trying to win arguments with people who don't have the same vision as you. They don't have the same vantage point you have. The Victims, The Complainers, and The Demanders might find attention, but they'll never find success.

6

THE HERO CODE

Definition of the word - Hero = a person admired or idealized for courage, outstanding achievements, or noble qualities.

MAKE YOUR BED

The year: 2014. The place: The University of Texas. The Occasion: Commencement speech to the graduates. The invited speaker, U.T. alumnus Admiral William H. McRaven, stood in front of the podium and gave a speech that went viral. I recommend watching it on YouTube if you have yet to hear it. It's a wise way to spend 19 minutes and twenty-seven seconds of your life, especially when you compare it to other ways you kill time.

Admiral McRaven admonished the graduates and the world not to belittle or disregard simple tasks. On the contrary, he stated that to be successful in life, start with the little tasks. Start with making your bed. When you get up in the morning, you have a choice to make; you can make your bed or keep it messy. As an Admiral for the Navy Seals, the world's most elite fighting force, he, probably more than anyone, understands the power of momentum.

He said that if you decide to leave your bed a mess, it begins the trajectory of your day. You've started on the negative, already failing the first task of the day. However, if you decide to make your bed first thing in the morning, you have conquered the first task of the day. You've already accomplished something, and starting with good momentum is a preferable way to start your day. That will put you in a better position to handle whatever comes next.

I mention this because in order for you to be successful and say, 'Failure is not an option,' remember to do the little things. Business owners tend to be visionaries; we love to think about the company's future success. We have no problem writing out our 1-year, 5-year, and 10-year goals. We'll share the visions of our great futures. And when the time comes to make them happen, we brace up to tackle the mountains that stand in our way. The many people who fail are the ones who forget the details, the little things. It's as if they're so excited to create a massive stage they can stand on that they order the materials and put it all together but forget to nail the pieces together. You will not reach the highest levels of life jumping off an unsteady foundation.

In short, make your bed, do the little things, and set yourself up for success for the rest of the day.

Do that consistently and set yourself up for success for the rest of your life.

THE HERO CODE

Since that speech, Admiral McRaven has been on many more stages and has written four books. As of this writing, his most recent book is *The Hero Code: Lessons Learned From Lives Well Lived*, published in 2021. In it, he honors people he deems as heroes and writes about qualities within them that make them heroes. He gathered their distinct characteristics and mashed them together to create what he calls, the Hero Code.

Courage:

It takes courage to say F*ck Failure just once, let alone every morning. Many people don't understand what it means to be courageous. Since each views the world centered on their perspectives, the definitions of courage vary. This is why being courageous or defining an act of courage takes many shapes and forms. For some, it's climbing a tree to save a cat or having the fortitude to jump out of a perfectly functioning airplane, and for others, it means being like Rambo, defeating an entire army by yourself. In short, courage is the ability to do something that frightens you.

I'm afraid of heights. If you put me in a high location and I see the solid ground far below me, my heart races and my palms might get slightly clammy. I don't like it. I recently saw a guy walking on a solo beam 20 feet off the ground without a rope or support should he fall. He did what he had to do at that altitude, then squatted down on the beam, put his hands on it, and jumped, landing safely on the grass. To me, that's courageous. To him, it was something he did on a Tuesday afternoon that he'd never even remember.

Some people I know are scared to get out of bed every morning, and it takes great courage for them to get up and face the day. For some, it could be because of what the day holds for them, and others suffer from one form of anxiety or another. The next person you talk to could have to summon up all the courage they can muster because they suffer from social anxiety. One never knows what others go through, which is why everyone should be treated with respect and dignity. To those of you who face your fears, even if it's getting out of bed in going after the life you want to live, I applaud you.

Thus far in this book, I've mentioned several fears – fear of success, failure, moments of insanity vs. moments of clarity, fear of losing money, opportunities, fears of making bad decisions, choosing the wrong partner, and more. I'm here to tell you that the road to success, however you define success to be, leads to and through fear.

Find the courage to get through the other side of fear and watch it diminish in your rearview mirror.

Be strong and courageous; screw failure!

Humility:

I've been called many good, not-so-good, and horrible names. In my heart, I'm a humble, very appreciative man. However, many times, what comes out of my mouth is anything but humility.

I'm a little Old School. I expect people to do their jobs; after all, it's what they get paid to do. I've always made it a point to take personal responsibility for my actions. That way of thinking was emphasized and wedged into me more when I served in the United States Marine Corps. You were expected to show up on time, do your job right, get out and stay out of trouble until it was time to show up on time the next day. You don't get thanked or applauded for doing that. It's a simple matter of you living up to your part of the deal with the corps. As much as you don't thank them when they pay you for what you've earned, you don't get thanked for doing what you agreed to do to get paid.

I will admit to you that I have big goals and dreams and that I want to make big moves to help my family become financially independent while being of service and helping others. In saying that, often, my humility tends to get overshadowed by a sense of cockiness, or it comes across as arrogance. I can sometimes come across as quite the asshole, according to my wife, Jennyffer, because I'm a big-picture guy and can't stand people's lame excuses or laziness and will often say it. If I've come across that way with you, please bear with me; I, too, am a work in progress.

Admiral McRaven, on the other hand, has the humility thing down pat. He states that humility is born of respect: respect for ourselves, respect for others, respect for what we don't know, and respect for what we readily see.

I love his quote on humility:

"I'll work to be humble, to recognize the limits of my intellect,

understanding, and power."

44

— ADMIRAL WILLIAM H. MCRAVEN

In my naivety, I thought I could do it all by myself. I felt that I could dream it and do it because I'm not afraid to put the work in to get it. I got to the point where I couldn't do any more by myself. I had to humble myself and realize I needed help. I realized that, yes, I was good, but not that good to live the life I wanted without help from others. That single moment of clarity helped me achieve things I could never have done independently.

To not fail, don't be afraid or too proud to ask for help. Don't be intimidated to hire people that are smarter than you. Don't worry about admitting you don't know what to do next. Don't be too proud not to seek guidance. If you're not humble and you're constantly bragging, you'll leave no room for others to say good things about you.

Also, as my wife would tell you, don't hog all the credit; be humble enough to thank those who helped you get to where you are, and they'll help you get to where you want to be.

Humility is priceless.

<u>Sacrifice:</u>

Winning anything competitive takes sacrifice. Living your dream life requires sacrifice, usually in the form of time, comfort, or money. Depending on what success means to you, sacrifice means different things to different people. To have rock-hard abs and a smoking-hot body, you must sacrifice foods you enjoy and put your body through the workout process, endure the pain as your muscles heal, abstain or limit your alcohol intake, and get plenty of sleep. If you want a great degree of financial success, you may have to sacrifice family time, first steps, baseball games or cheerleading tryouts, two-week vacations, and other time-consuming habits that would hinder you.

Actions of sacrifice have many benefits. For one, it helps us get to where we want to. But secondly, and equally as important, when we give our time, talent, and treasure to others, it makes us better as a people. This is why I give away my secrets when I get on stages. As a human being, it's essential for me to give back. Too many people try to hide what they've done to be successful, which is shameful and greedy to me.

I'm often asked why I would give away my secret sauce to a room full of people who could be deemed competitors. I always answer the same way:

90% of the people listening aren't willing to do the work necessary to get to where I am. 5% will do precisely what I've done, and good for them, they deserve it. The remaining 5% will do what I've done, tweak things to their style, and far surpass anything I've done.

I hope they turn around and tell me what they did differently so I can continue to step up my game.

There are people we call heroes in our world, and then there are actual, bonafide heroes. Their level of sacrifice cannot be measured by money or fame. In the book *The Hero Code*, Admiral McRaven tells the story of Ralph Johnson, born January 11, 1949, in Charlestown, South Carolina. Mr. Johnson was an African-American who grew up in tumultuous, racial times, to say the least. He willingly joined the Marine Corps during the Vietnam War; he wasn't forced through the draft - he chose to defend his country, as imperfect as it was.

While serving as a reconnaissance scout with his group of 15 men, they were attacked by a platoon-sized group (32-50 soldiers) of the North Vietnamese Army and Viet Cong forces in the early morning hours. Private First Class Johnson was in a three-person fighting hole alongside two other Marines when a live hand grenade landed in their midst. Realizing the inherent danger to his two comrades, he shouted a warning and, without hesitation, hurled himself on the explosive device. His body absorbed the impact of the blast and was killed instantly. The other two men survived the battle directly due to his selfless devotion, courage, and sacrifice.

I relay that story so that you can see your sacrifice with a different lens. No need to cry, "Woe is me!" Some people have sacrificed everything so that you have the luxury of offering your time to get what you want.

You have to be willing to sacrifice today to have the future life of your dreams. If a car is the vehicle to get you where you want to go, sacrifice is the gas. You have to feed your vision and ambition with consistent sacrifice.

Integrity:

This is one of the most significant characteristics of the Hero Code. If you don't have integrity in my world, you don't stay in business for long. I have learned the hard way when I hire people to choose integrity over personality and charisma. At the end of the day, if you don't have integrity, you're not a good person. I choose who I work with, go to battle with, and get in the trenches with. Winning is complicated enough on its own than trying to win with liars, cheaters, and thieves punching holes in your ship. Surround yourself with people of integrity and hold yourself to a high level of integrity.

A true saying in business was first said by Bob Burg, the author of Endless Referrals – "All things being equal, people will do business with and refer business to people they know, like, and trust."

Today, more than ever, you need to get people to feel as if they know, like, and trust you. The Know part is why Grant Cardone says, "Money follows attention." If people don't know you, they can't support you. The Like part has to do with your personality, with genuinely trying to engage as a human being with another human being instead of being a salesperson trying to close a deal. The Trust part has to do with integrity.

I don't care who you are and how smoothly you speak; if people don't trust you, you'll never come close to reaching your potential. That is why, as of late, I've been stressing the importance of the video message to my team and my coaching clients. In a text, people don't see or hear you. They listen to you in a voicemail or phone call but don't see you. However, they can listen to you and see you by leaving a video message.

Then, when you meet in person and shake their hands, you are 66% there to get them to know, like, and trust you. The human connection is vital in making people feel they can trust you.

Someone once said integrity is doing the right thing even when no one is looking. If you conduct yourself with integrity, whether people see it or not, it will reveal itself sooner or later. It will shroud you like good karma, and better opportunities will come your way.

At the end of the day, you have no choice but to live with yourself. You can either be in a mansion, living with regret because you lied to people and screwed them over, or in an estate, at peace with yourself because you didn't lose your moral compass and didn't resort to lying, cheating, or stealing. Which person would you rather be?

Perseverance:

To persevere means never giving up on what matters to you. That sums up the core message of this book. It's just a different way of saying, F*ck Failure. Never allow the circumstances of your life, work, home, or anyone else to put your dreams into a corner to curl up and die. To quote the late, great Patrick Swayze in Dirty Dancing, "No one puts Baby in a corner." If you continue to fight, you haven't lost. If you're lying on the mat, struggling to get up, you haven't failed. Persevere with everything you have to never give up on the life you design for yourself.

I will share with you the secret to persevere, regardless of the situation. It's not a fancy, deep-thought, life hack. Ready? Here it is. **Be consistent.** That's it. Just be consistent.

Keep waking up, keep making your bed, keep your eyes on the prize, keep getting up when you get knocked down, keep celebrating wins, keep yourself surrounded by intelligent people and people who encourage you, keep serving others, keep looking for better ways and techniques to do what you do better, keep staying true to your why. Stay consistent in having honor, courage, and commitment, which is the Marine Corps motto. You can't fail if you persevere.

Duty:

When it comes to saying F*ck Failure and the responsibility of one's success, Grant Cardone says, "Success is your DUTY, obligation, and responsibility."

Your finances and health are your responsibilities. If you're struggling financially, sorry, but it's your fault. If you're obese, sorry, but it's your fault (unless you genuinely have a medical reason). However, I'll take it further: it's your duty to lift others around you. It's your duty to do what you can to create a better world for the next generation. Sadly, people use the word, Duty, like a hot potato, trying to pass it on to someone else.

It is your duty to do the job you get paid to do. It doesn't matter if it's a 9-to-5 office job, if you're a UPS driver, an assembly-line worker for Amazon, a school custodian, or a school principal. You have entered into an agreement that it is your duty to do the job they pay you to do. If you're an employee, that duty ends when your shift ends. It's not your duty to take someone else's problems home with you and add stress that you pass on to your family. If you're a business owner, that's different.

It is a business owner's duty to do whatever it takes to make the business profitable. Otherwise, you're skirting your duties, and the ramifications will manifest in disaster for the company. Your first duty is to yourself. It's like when someone is on an airplane going through massive turbulence and the air masks deploy – the flight attendant instructs you to use the oxygen mask on yourself first; otherwise, you won't be able to help others.

As you're searching for success, make sure to take care of yourself first. That is not being selfish. That is setting yourself up to grow a business that can provide for your family. Once you've established that foundation, it becomes your duty to grow the business to employ others, in essence, to feed and shelter others.

It is your duty to make money. How can you support other businesses, the topics you are passionate about, and your community if you don't make money? You should have a burning desire to make money, not for a fancy car or big title, but to be of more help to others. Successful people donate to causes bigger than themselves. I urge you to be a giver, not a taker. Givers are what make the world go around. They strive to make much so they can positively impact many. Takers are at their homes, receiving (not earning) a paycheck for doing nothing.

"I can't help the poor if I'm one of them.

So, I got rich and gave back. To me, that's the win-win."

— LYRICS FROM JAY-Z, AKA SEAN CARTER

It is your duty to be a contributing member of society. It is your duty to play by the rules. As a former Marine, duty and responsibility were ingrained in me, and I had no chance but to either play by their code or get ousted unceremoniously. It is your duty to be a good spouse. It is your duty to be a good parent. No one can do those things for you. If you don't do them, your entire existence is just sad. Take a 360-degree look at your life and ensure you fulfill your obligations. If you are, you'll be far from failure and much closer to success.

<u>Forgiveness:</u>

"No matter how great or small the offense,

I will forgive.

I will be the victor and not the victim."

— ADMIRAL WILLIAM H. MCRAVEN

Businesses and goals bring with them warranted bucketloads of stress and responsibilities. It is foolish to carry on additional weight willingly. Unforgiveness is a weight that can drown people in anger, resentment, and sorrow – a flower cannot grow in that type of field. If people go after you on social media –Thumb Warriors who talk a big game behind their screen – that's on them. The more you succeed, the more Facebook and Twitter villains will pop up – some out of nowhere and others from your inner circle. You can't stop them from feeling the way they want to feel and talking bad about you – but you can stop yourself from focusing on it and letting it rob you of your energy.

I'm not saying to stand pat and let people screw you over; I'm saying don't let bullcrap you have no control over linger inside of you that will limit your success by taking up your precious time.

Even though I'm half Jewish, I feel obligated to quote Jesus regarding forgiveness. He famously said, "Forgive them, for they know not what they do." He was talking about the very people who whipped and beat him and ultimately killed him in the cruelest way possible. Regardless of anyone's religious belief, it cannot be disputed that Jesus was perhaps the single most significant leader or influencer in the history of humankind. Our very calendar – B.C. and A.C. – centers on his existence. If we can learn things from Elon Musk and others, I think it's fair to say we can learn things from Jesus.

When it comes to someone doing you wrong, though, forgiving is easier said than done. In no way am I a saint, but I have learned to forgive. My former best friend and the best man at my wedding had an issue with me, but instead of approaching me to talk about it, he sought to destroy my reputation through social media. In my mind, I couldn't care – the energy it would take did not align with me becoming the best version of myself I'm desperately working to be. I didn't retort, and I didn't say negative things about him on social media. That type of energy does not align with my goals. He has the God-given right to feel the way he does. At the end of the day, I quelled my anger and forgave him. Whatever pain he feels I put on him, I hope he can forgive me too.

Another former business associate decided to sue me and put my family, my business, and me in a difficult financial situation. He attempted to take food away from my table and changed my trajectory from going upwards to pivoting into a downward spiral. For some reason, he morphed his insecurities about making it on his own into the form of a frivolous lawsuit. He has his reasons. Whether they are good or bad intentions, truths or fabrications and exaggerations – I can't let it matter to me anymore.

The plan my wife and I have for our lives is bigger than the remorse and anger that, left unchecked, would consume us.

So I forgave him. And trust me, this one was not easy to do. It took work. I might still be working on it from time to time.

Dear reader, I urge you to do whatever is necessary but find a way to forgive. Unleash yourself from the burden of negativity. The person or people you have not forgiven probably don't even think about you or the incident anymore. They've moved on with their lives while you've stayed emotionally stuck, unable to grow. Forgiving others frees you up for better emotions, better ways of thinking, and better opportunities.

Mostly, forgive yourself.

Forgive yourself for all the dumb stuff you've done. Forgive yourself for the ridiculous things you've said and for mistreating others. Today is a new day. Tomorrow is yours to invent. Your future is waiting for you. Play by the Hero's Code and be a real-life hero.

❼

INNOVATE OR STAGNATE

FEED YOUR MIND

I workout in the morning at least four days a week. I don't always get to do it, especially when traveling but it's an important part of my mind, body, and soul, self-care routine. I workout for several reasons. Obviously, it's to stay healthy, it's also to justify the sifter of whiskeys and medium rare steaks I enjoy, but also, and just as importantly as the health aspect of it, I get out of the house to train and detach from the world and think/meditate on things or to listen to pumped up music, stimulating podcasts or audiobooks.

The morning of this particular writing, I was listening to a podcast on innovation. It wasn't something that randomly came through my headphones, I purposely searched for it since I'm a big believer that if you don't innovate, you stagnate. One of the things that perplexes me is that there is so much free information out there, yet so many people fail at so many things, whether it's business, relationships, money management, their health or even how to bake a cake. I don't understand why people don't consume free content that can make them better should they apply what they learn.

As it relates to business, innovation is critical.

A company can do everything right, hire the right people, put together the right strategies, and make a ton of money. However, if they don't keep their head on a swivel and identify new areas of innovation, no matter how big they've gotten, they too can fail. Especially when a market goes through a shift affecting business and consumers.

You may recall the app called, Vine. It was founded in 2012 and took the social media world by storm with its 6-second, looping videos, often to hilarious effects. When other sites included similar features, the Vine executives didn't innovate anything new and it died in just 4 years. Other companies, behemoths such as Kodak and Blockbuster didn't see or care to see the innovations of digital photography and streaming movies and they too went out of business. The list goes on and on with companies such as Pier 1 Imports, Borders, Sports Authority, Solyndra – a solar panel manufacturing company that despite making $140 million in revenue couldn't compete with the influx of cheaper solar panels. Dress Barn, Toys R Us, American Apparel, Lord & Taylor, all retail companies that went out of business before the pandemic because of their outdated systems and business practices.

There are many different ways on being successful in business, but at the core, it's really just these four things:

1. You need the courage to start it or buy it. (Taking a risk)
2. You need to see what your competitors are doing and not doing. (Study your competitors)
3. You need to find out the needs of your prospects. (Knowing your market)
4. You need to implement the plan you devise once you know the answers to questions 2 and 3. (Taking ACTION)

If you don't do these four things, your company will rest in peace alongside the ones I just mentioned.

I get it. You may not want to try to build the next Toyota, Tesla, Apple, or Amazon. Maybe you started your business because you're passionate about it and you just want to make a good living while being your own boss. Kudos to you if that's what success is to you. You go with your bad self. Even if that is the case, you too need to be aware of the need to innovate because whether you're a big company or a sole proprietor, fundamental business laws apply to all and it doesn't matter how cute you are, if you don't follow them, you'll get swallowed up by those that do. I'm excited about this chapter because I'm not just going to share with you that you should be open to innovation, I'm going to guide and teach you on *how* to be innovative. Ready? Let's roll.

INNOVATION

Ask yourself:

What's my value proposition?

Who are the people I serve?

How am I innovating to attract more attention to get more people to want to work with me?

The real estate industry has to be one of the biggest revolving doors in terms of industry. Thousands of people get into real estate thinking it can't be too difficult to sell a home. Thousands of people have left the industry with their tails between their legs because they realized that there is a lot of competition here, only the strong survive. The good thing about this industry is that information is everywhere and the ones who absolutely crush it leave golden nuggets anyone can find. Clues to success are as easy to find as the turn-by-turn GPS directions on your phone. So long as you follow your GPS, you'll get to your destination. Similarly, as long as you follow what the successful people do – and put in the work required – you'll be successful.

I love it when new real estate agents tell me they plan to be the #1 realtor in their area. Don't get me wrong, I love the swagger, but wanting something still leaves you a million miles away from getting it. You can want all you want but if you don't do it, you won't get it. I ask them, "How do you plan to be different?" They usually stumble with the answer because they don't know it. I answer it for them. "You need to be innovative."

I joke with agents all the time and tell them,

"If you want to be innovative, start with picking up the phone every time it rings!"

I don't understand why sales professionals don't answer their phones. Although there's some humor to it, a professional that gets known for always being available to their clients, including evenings and weekends, gets ahead of the game. No matter what business you may be in, if you serve others, as silly or simple as it sounds, pick up the phone – every time! Perhaps you need to change your mindset and instead of thinking you're being bothered or interrupted by a phone call, understand that you're getting blessed with an opportunity to make money.

I'LL HAVE WHAT SHE'S HAVING

Studying your competition is key. Some people study their competition so they can be like them; others try to know their competition so they can do what they do, but better, to destroy them. It doesn't matter to me why you study the competition, just do it. The trick is to study ones that are doing much better than you. It makes no sense to put time and effort into studying those like you, and the only time to study someone worse than you is when you're at the top of the ladder and want to make sure you notice what others who are starting to catch up are doing.

Whatever you pick up from your competitors, the secret sauce is to give it your unique flair to make it yours. In other words, you don't have to innovate to the point that you're reinventing the wheel, just take something that's working and innovate it to your style and personality. If you can take a sound business practice and make it yours, over time people will realize it and want to work with you more. Studying the competition is extremely important when it comes to business planning, but I'll dive deep into that in the following chapter.

Another thing I tell my clients is to do your own market research. Yes, I know that there are many sites and systems with statistics, but nothing will get you known in the area you serve by conducting your own market research.

I have often recommended my real estate agent clients knock on 200 doors and get their own data. Just knock on a door and say, "Hello, my name is David, I'm a realtor in your area but I'm not here to try to sell you anything. Can I ask you three quick questions?"

1. What did you love about the agent that helped you get this house?
2. What did you dislike about the process or the agent?
3. Do you remember the agent's name?

If you do that, the people who will talk to you will see how you're genuinely trying to provide your clients with the best service possible, without you selling yourself. It's amazing how many homeowners don't recall their agent. The reason being is that the relationship with that person was transactional, not relational.

Three amazing things will come from this type of market analysis.

1. People may tell you they are in the process of buying or selling and want you to be their agent, or they may know someone in the market and they'll refer you.
2. You'll be able to put together a plan based on real-time statistics in your area and not make a plan based on national average statistics that might not mean shit where you live.
3. You might get chased off of a property by an old man with a shotgun and be able to share some hilarious stories with your friends.

Companies like Apple and Tesla send out surveys to millions of people via email, most small companies don't have that luxury. But that doesn't mean that some good, old-fashioned hard work can't get you the information you need. For example, if you're planning on opening up an

Italian restaurant, a pet grooming store, or a side-hustle t-shirt business, the same principles apply. Knock on 200 doors that surround your business, let people know about your restaurant, ask them what type of Italian foods they like, and tell them your unique story. There may already be 4 different Italian restaurants selling spaghetti in the vicinity but even if they've been around for years, you've gained a serious competitive advantage because everyone you touched and everyone you've spoken with will come to your restaurant simply because of the two-minute conversation that created a relationship.

This is how you stand out in a crowded marketplace. This is how you tell your story. Prospects will feel vested in you because they'll feel that they had an itty-bitty hand in how you do business. There are so many people on social media – LinkedIn, Instagram, Twitter (X), Facebook, Tik Tok, so many people sending out mailers, so many people with websites, business cards, and logos – but nothing, and I mean nothing beats personal, face-to-face, eye-to-eye, handshaking contact.

MENTORSHIP

I respect the mentor/mentee relationship. To be clear, a mentor isn't your best friend that you discuss your love life with or a colleague that's going through the same shit you are. A mentor is someone that is more successful than you, someone who has gotten to where you want to go or to where you want to surpass. He or she has chosen to spend time pouring their knowledge and advice into you. Having a great mentor is a business hack. It's one of the ways to grow exponentially in a short amount of time.

You can learn valuable lessons that took 20 years to learn in 20 minutes. If you're a good mentee and can put into practice the do's and not do the don'ts, apply your own seasoning to make it yours, and you have a bright future ahead of you. However, I can't speak too much on being a mentee because I never had a person I considered a mentor.

I don't know if it was because I started off the gate running and never looked back, or if I gave the impression that I didn't need or want any help, or if people saw my rise and figured if they helped me I'd take over the whole damn city. Either way, I did not have the luxury of being a mentee. I wish I did. I wish I could point at someone and say thank you for taking the time to instruct me, you helped make me.

As a result, I probably had more hiccups than the average person. However, I was resolute in wanting to be successful, so I invented my own mentors, and you can too.

I began following the greats, the gurus, from around the country and world. I didn't vibe with everyone, but people that I've already mentioned like Grant, Gary V, Elon Musk, and others opened up my mind and opened up my openness to limitless possibilities. Thankfully as I write this book I find myself with potentially two mentors in my life. Two amazing people who started from nothing and are now billionaires. I tell you this to let you know, it's never too late to find a mentor and it's always good to have one. Before that, to enhance my education and reach, I began to go to conferences, big ones and small ones. I would go for the knowledge – I would see what was on the agenda and attend the ones where I needed the most help. However, the main reason why I would go was for the connections.

In 2020 - 2021, most conferences were virtual, in this post pandemic world. It would be much easier to sit in my pajamas behind a screen and get the same knowledge as if I were in the front row, but the reason why I buy the plane ticket, rental car, hotel, food is to mingle with people. People that attend conferences tend to be highly motivated individuals, like myself. The connections I've made have catapulted my career. At first I would go to conferences, then I started getting asked to participate and speak at conferences, and then I started throwing the biggest real estate conferences in Miami, New Jersey, Orlando, New York and more.

I also go to masterminds. That's usually a small group of like-minded people that discuss their business issues and the others give them feedback and identify blind spots the person doesn't see. Just as I would attend a conference, I'll jump on a plane for the right mastermind session. I've flown across the country to attend a very expensive mastermind in Southern California with some very high net worth individuals.

It was worth every penny. Miami is as competitive a market for real estate as there is in the country.

Getting out of the bubble in Miami, seeing what others are doing successfully in other areas is one of the reasons I stay ahead of the competition.

When I go to some masterminds, I listen and take notes more than I talk. I already know what I know; I'm there to find out things I don't know.

It was in California where I met someone who had a YouTube channel and his own podcast. I asked him a lot of questions of the pros and cons as it related to his time and effort vs. his return on investment and time. What you have to understand about putting out content is that it's a marketing play and sometimes you can't quantify it in dollars. However, it raises your profile; and the attention and credibility you get is all a part of the success sandwich.

More than financial return on investment (ROI) they see more of a return on time (ROT).

I flew back to Miami and soon after I started my YouTube channel and podcast.

Speaking of YouTube and Podcasts, don't sleep on the information you can get there. There are straight killers giving away amazing, real-time advice. At the time of this writing, an audio only app called Clubhouse had made a name for itself. The app allows you to "enter a room" and listen to conversations of topics you're interested in. I have popped into "rooms" and exited out with vigorously taken notes that I've put my spin on and shared with my team. The app is no longer as popular as it was, but many people have lost out on valuable, free information on it. As time continues, more, even better apps will be developed. My point is to take advantage of whatever technology exists to either receive or give information.

Reading is fundamental to growth. Someone once said that the wealthy hide their secrets in books because the poor wont find them there. I'm a big advocate for reading industry-related books or books that can strengthen your mindset. At times people have told me that they can't read for long because it makes them sleepy. There's a reason for that. If you never do squats but go to the gym and do squats, your legs would be sore, you'd feel the soreness when you go up stairs. Why? Because your legs are a muscle and they're not used to that much exertion. Guess what? The eye is a muscle too! People who don't read have weak eyes. I advise them to start with a few pages and then put the book down. Once you get the hang of that, read some more pages. Then, read a chapter, and then read two chapters. After a while, if the book is good enough, you'll find that you wished you had more time to read.

Books have changed the world.

There is no one that can convince me that books like the Torah, Bible, or Quran didn't change the course of human history. Much more light-hearted and recent, the Harry Potter books also made their mark on the world. Nothing is more powerful than words on paper and eyes on paper and eyes hitting the brain with knowledge.

To sum this chapter up, there are many ways to innovate, to make something unique to you. Just as with everything else, you have to want to put in the work. If you do, who knows, maybe someone will write a book about you one day.

8

THE ENTREPRENEUR'S STANDARD OPERATING PROCEDURE

The history of humanity is as redundant as it is impressive. As a species, our technological advancements have surpassed expectations, although I thought we'd have flying cars in use by now. Still, handheld computers (phones) now cover more data than entire computer labs that took up an entire floor. Also, we've developed a new, purely digital currency that has real-world value, the metaverse allows us to submerse ourselves in an entirely different world, and we will soon colonize the moon and then, Mars. So, as a species, we are on a roll!

However, we've also forgotten many things. The Egyptians have forgotten how they built pyramids. The Romans have forgotten how they created the aqueducts that enabled them to have the mightiest city, perhaps of all time. There are also many tried and true remedies and sciences that worked amazingly well before but the knowledge of constructing it has not made it to this generation.

This is why I say, it's important to have your S.O.P. – Standard Operating Procedures.

By having everything down in writing, as I'm doing for you in this book, nothing gets forgotten and you can continue to add to your skill sets instead of adding and subtracting as I've illustrated in the start of this chapter. Let's face it; if your mama or grandmamma doesn't hand down her recipe, your favorite dish will disappear like the pyramids.

I'm big on SOPs. It started when I was in the Marine Corps. I could get stationed at any base around the world, go into the armory, pull out the Standard Operating Procedures book, and if it were properly updated, I wouldn't need anyone to train me or tell me what to do. I have SOPs for just about everything in my business, which is one of the reasons why I believe it continues to grow.

The problem for many business people is that they are often not prepared to run a business – they either grow too fast or they take over a business that hasn't been structured optimally, so they're not running them efficiently. If you're a CEO, President, Manager of a business, or a solo-preneur with ambitions of expansion, can you imagine how much easier and smoother it would be if you could hand new hires an SOP book? How much more time would you have? How much more efficient would you be? How much more likely is it that things will be done right, and done right the first time?

In an effort to make sure you take away some tangible take-aways, here's the Entrepreneurs SOP.

IT STARTS WITH DEVELOPING YOUR WHY!

As humans, we need a reason to wake up every morning. Otherwise, it's a mundane existence and no one I want to know wants to live a less than average, boring, and monotonous life. For people with drive and ambition, we need to know why the efforts of the day ahead are important. Your soul needs to know why.

I know my why. It motivates me to get out of the bed at 5 AM every morning. I make sure to be at the gym at 5:30 for "ME" Time. If you can be completely honest with yourself and dig through the real and fake humility, and get to the core of what makes you tick and what you truly want out of life – the answer will make you change your habits so that you get it.

Your why provides the fuel to the plan of your attack for your business life. It helps you with your yes's and no's:

"Yes, I'd love to go to the networking event, thanks for inviting me."

"Sorry, but no, I don't have time to play 18 holes of golf with your sorority brothers on a Wednesday, but thanks for inviting me."

Discovering your why is a journey unto itself. If you can blurt out your why, chances are you're not digging deep enough to what makes you tick. This is how that conversation with my coach went.

"David, why do you work so hard and with so much passion?"

I answered, "I want to provide for my family." In my head, *'duh, doesn't everybody?'*

Then, she asked, "What does that mean?"

"I want to 10X their lives now so that they don't suffer and go without as much as I did as a child."

"I get that," she asked. "Why is that important?"

She had a follow up question for each answer, and every question was either - why is that important to you, or why? In my head, I was like, *how annoying are you going to be? It's like talking to a four-year-old and why the sky is blue. I don't know...*

That's when the realization came to me. I did know. I had the answer to my why all along; I just never dug deep enough to get it.

This is how to create your S.O.Ps – get a piece of paper and write down your why. That's right; write it down with a pen and your hand. Why do you wake up every day? If you're not where you want to be in your life, write down why you're reading this book. Why are you seeking self-development instead of binge-watching shows on Netflix right now? If you have children, they are most likely your why, but go a layer deeper. Why? When you have that answer, dig in deeper, and deeper, and deeper.

To ensure that you get to the real you, understand that it is 100% okay to be selfish. If your why turns out that you want to prove someone wrong, or that you want to do better than your older sister that used to beat you at everything and embarrass you, or that you want to show your ex-spouse that she or she should have never left you, or that you want to be famous, - that's okay. Your why is not going to get voted on or judged. It's not even to be shared should you not want to. Your why is a one-on-one exercise with the only person that can give you the life you deserve – yourself.

How would your life change if you lived up to the best version of yourself?

How does that make you feel? What would happen to the people you love if you're continuously and conscientiously trying to be your best self? How high can the best YOU climb? I think it's time to find your authentic why. It's the only thing that can make you go after the best life you can live.

My why is FREEDOM. It's a simple word, and it has different meanings for different people. But ultimately, I am building a business that allows me to do whatever I want. That might sound selfish or egotistical to you, but I'm not you, I'm me. I don't want to work till I'm 90 or even 65. I want to be able to go on vacation whenever the heck I want. I want to have the right people at the right seat on the train of my company, fully trained and motivated and making money, so that I can work when I want and play when I want. I want my wife to know that she married a stud, a man that can provide her the lifestyle of her dreams. I want my kids to see that I busted my ass and, even though I've had setbacks, I never gave up and now they are benefitting from the audacious vision I had of myself and they can enjoy fruits of my labor while still having serious work-ethic to reach their own goals. I want my wife and kids to be extremely proud of me. For me, that sums up to freedom. Financial freedom, location freedom, family freedom, time freedom, etc.

When I get out of bed in the morning and put my feet on the ground, I say, with a sleepy, raspy voice, "It's a Freedom Day."

Freedom is fought for. Freedom is died for. The quest for it pushes me, corrects me, punishes me, rewards me, enlightens me, and continually fills me with the desire to not live an average life.

I can't stress enough the importance of this exercise. Dig in until it embarrasses you. If you're not afraid of yourself to unlock the true desire of your heart, you'll awaken a passion and drive that you never knew you had. The secret to your ultimate happiness and success is found in finding your why.

THE 5-3-1 EXERCISE

This is your 5 year, 3 year, and 1 year vision of yourself. Where do you expect to be in 5, 3 and 1 years? Who do you become? In what ways have you changed?

I don't like to envision myself more than 5 years from now. A friend of mine used to have 1, 5, and 10-year goals. Then, he almost died from Stage 3 throat cancer. He now does the 5-3-1-goal exercise. When I asked him why, he said, "When I was at death's door as I battled cancer, I realized that tomorrow is not promised. If I focus on more immediate goals, I'll get to those ultimate goals too."

If you can visualize yourself in a year, three years, and five years, meaning, you can visualize the coordinates of your life, you can reverse engineer how to get there. It's a lot easier getting to a place you've never been with correct GPS coordinates than by spontaneously heading out on a trip with the plan of asking strangers for directions along the way.

Once you understand your why, this exercise is a little easier. Don't get it twisted; this is a different exercise than finding your why. Your why is internal to you, your thoughts, your emotions, your upbringing, traumatic events that you may have gone through, and other things that are uniquely personal to you. The 5-3-1 is more about the outside of you.

For you, you may be retired in 5 years or you see yourself vacationing on an amazing beach in Puerto Rico or Tahiti. You may be closing on your home in North Carolina or on your farm in Idaho. I just have to believe that if you're reading this book, you don't want to be where you are now, five years from now.

Again, at no point did I say to type out or put into the Notes section of your phone – I said to WRITE IT OUT. At the top of the page, write:

5 YEARS FROM TODAY!

Then, close your eyes and allow your mind and your why to come together. Envision your best life 5 years from now. What car will you drive? Where will you live? Are you happily married, happily single, or happily divorced? Do you have kids? If so, what cars are they driving, what schools are they going to, and what did you buy them for Christmas that year? How much are you making in profit – ten thousand a month, 50 thousand a month or a million dollars a day?

Then, do the same exercise. At the top of the page, write:

3 YEARS FROM TODAY!

You'll notice that you're not thinking as big. Reality starts to creep in and you assess more where you are than the vision of where you dream to be. But do the same exercise. Answer the same questions as before. You can also add other questions – are you still Ubering? Did you get your real estate license? Have you found a location for your second restaurant? Did you move to Texas, California, or Florida? Did you pull the trigger on the dog?

Then, do the same exercise. At the top of the page, write:

1 YEAR FROM TODAY!

This is when things get real. 12 months goes by fast. If you're over the age of 35, you understand how fast time flies. Before you know it, you're planning your next birthday even though you're still recovering from your previous birthday. If you're in your 20s, how fast was high school? Didn't those 4 years fly by?

Your one-year goals are certainly not nearly as grandiose as your five-year goals. But your five year goals, along with your why, is what gives you the sense of commitment to do what you need to do today, tomorrow, and next week to become the person you can envision.

Now, you can change the questions up a bit and ask yourself:

What do I need to do today? Who do I need to meet? What class or course or certification do I need to subscribe to right now? What habits do I have to stop or control – drinking, over-sleeping, spending, over-eating, drug use, etc.?

The road to a thousand miles begins with one step.

By doing these two invasive, personal, yet simple exercises, you'll be on the road to getting to where you want to be. The side effect is immediate though. Being that you've aligned with what your future looks like and you're making the necessary moves to get there – your quality of life will improve immediately. You'll find joy in the process because you know it's bringing you somewhere. Instead of being frustrated thinking, *I'll never live the life I want!* your self-esteem will grow knowing that you are now doing exactly what needs to be done to get the life you want.

That's it. Super simple. All you have to do is want it.

9

GO AHEAD, MAKE MORE MONEY

I'd be willing to wager that one of the reasons, if not the biggest reason, why you're reading this book is so that you can make more money. It's okay if it is. One of the reasons why I read books is so I can learn how to unblock my thoughts and/or actions so that I can be more loving (to myself and others), responsible, and, of course, more profitable. I'm assuming that you are much like me in that you want financial freedom also, so, Real-Talk, let's get into the Money-Talk.

FINANCIAL AFFIDAVIT

The purpose of a financial affidavit is to determine the income, assets, liabilities, and expenses of your business and personal life. You will never get your house in order if you can't truthfully evaluate your current income and expenses. If you allow yourself to live the lie that you don't spend more than you make, sooner or later, your credit card is going to get declined, you're going to get embarrassed, and you're going to get into major debt. In short, understanding your debt to income ratio will ultimately predict your future finances, so you better know it.

We live in a world filled with companies and services that entice us into automated monthly payments. It may not hurt you to lose $50-$200 a month on something you don't use anymore but forgot to cancel. However, if you're wasting $200 a month without getting a return of any kind, imagine how much better your business could be if you put another $2,400 a year into advertising and marketing your brand.

One of the life-saving survival tips of growing a profitable business is understanding how much you're spending, what you're spending the money on, and most importantly, what your return is on your investment (ROI). If you are investing an equal amount of money to all of your advertising/marketing channels, chances are, you're misusing your funds. There is no way that each channel is giving you the same return. You must (I said MUST, not SHOULD) figure out where you get the most ROI and allocate more funds to there if you want to become more profitable.

For instance, let's say you're purchasing leads from a particular company and for every ten leads you have a return of 3 or 4 times what you're spending, and to have a more varied approach, you're using a lead generating system that's giving you a zero to 1 times the investment; you might want to shut that one down and increase the amount of spend for the other lead generating company or evaluate why that one is not working.

As I write this, I think perhaps I shouldn't. Doesn't everybody know this? Isn't this common sense?

But then I remember that more than 80% of businesses crash and burn in the first five years and the biggest reason is that they never figured out how to manage their money.

So, let's go to Business Basics 101…

WHAT'S YOUR MONEY DOING FOR YOU?

Understanding your finances at a high-level does not require a CPA license. It's as simple as figuring out where your money is going and what you're getting back for it. If you're paying $1,000 a month for an assistant to make calls for you for 20 hours a week, and you're making

$4,000 a month in profit – you may want to figure out how you can pay him or her $2,000 or $3,000 a month so you convert that to $8,000 or $12,000 a month. Knowing how your money is working for you is critical to sustainable success.

I don't want to just tell you that you need to do it, I'm going to show you.

1. Calculate all the money that comes in on a monthly basis. If this is your first time doing it, don't just go by the previous month, start with six months back. Get your deposits and put them on a spreadsheet.
2. Calculate the cost of running your business – staff, rent, lights, dinners with potential clients, coffee meetings, CRM, online footprint (website, social media, newsletters, etc.), virtual assistants, clothing, branding, travel, - all of it!
3. Separate the income producing costs and the costs of doing business costs. For example, marketing, sales reps, coffee meetings are income producing costs. Rent, copier, gas and travel would be cost of doing business costs.
4. Go over each item and decide if you should put more resources into one, if you should put less in another, if you should cancel another one, or if you should add something you just realized your business is lacking.

I would also do this with your personal finances. It doesn't matter if you're single or married. It's up to you to figure out how you're going to pay your debts. If you do it right, it should determine if you're eating at a fancy restaurant on Saturday or putting a couple extra hundred dollars into a positive cash-generating lead flow. It could make the difference between spending $2,000 on bottles trying to look like a baller, or putting an extra $2,000 in your business in order to make $10,000 and get closer to actually becoming a baller.

I kept this part as simple and to the point as I could while ensuring you were getting tangible value. The secret to this is that you can't just look at this and think it's cool, or for you to shrug and tell yourself that while you don't know where every penny is going, you have a handle on it. I guess that's okay if you want to survive.

However, if you want to thrive and dominate the competition, do this exercise and hurdle the ones who think they've got it all figured out.

Elon Musk knew how much money he had when he started Space X. He had told his team that he only had enough money for three shuttle launches. The first launch failed. The second launch failed. The third launch failed. Elon didn't flinch. He spent every penny he could and they had a 4th launch. That launch got him a $1.5 billion contract with NASA. This was not budgeting! This was all risk. Today, he's the world's richest man. There are many reasons why – he's a visionary, he's a calculated risk-taker, and he knows his finances. I must confess, I too am willing to take calculated risks. When they fall, it stings. When they go right, it's usually a big payoff. Either way, the thrill and excitement of the ride is a reward on its own.

The problem for many entrepreneurs is that even though we strive hard for success, many of us don't know how to handle it when it comes trickling in. If you come from parents that never made more than $60K a year collectively, it's hard to learn how to manage a $150K year. There are people in serious financial trouble but continue to allow their spouse or kids to spend as much as they want. Do this exercise with your spouse, or even your kids, and teach them how to be financially literate. It's one of the best lessons you can teach. Become the one that changed generational financial illiteracy for your family. That's a boss move.

10

KNOW THYSELF AND KNOW OTHERS

KNOW THYSELF

In Act 1, Scene 3 of Shakespeare's play, *Hamlet,* a character by the name of Polonius gives his son a speech based on how to behave while at university. Within that speech, he famously says, *"To thine own self be true."* The entirety of that line goes like this,

> *"This above all: to thine own self be true, and it must follow, as the night the day. Thou canst not then be false to any man."*

I don't know if Shakespeare knew it when he wrote that line, but the manifestation of living it in real life is the lynchpin to success and happiness. The line ends up not being false (lying to, deceiving) others, but it's the beginning of the line with real power. Don't lie to yourself. In order to do that, you must know yourself.

Many tests give us an unbiased view as to who we are. My favorite by far is the DISC Profile and Personality Tests. It's a personal assessment tool used by more than a million people every year to help improve teamwork, communication, and productivity in the workplace. It is the best tool to deepen your understanding of yourself and others. It is used for self-awareness, improving teamwork, making conflict more productive, developing more vital sales skills, becoming a more effective manager/leader, and training without potential ramifications of preconceived judgments.

DISC is an acronym that stands for the four main personality traits in the model: D – Dominance, I – Influence, S – Steadiness, and C – Conscientiousness.

Not to state the obvious, but it's essential that you know your personality. Most people think of themselves as they would like to be, not who they are. Typically, people have an AH-HA moment when they get their test findings. This test is so thorough that it won't only tell you who you are privately, but if you act differently outside of your home, it'll let you know who you are publicly and show you why you behave differently. That could be a game-changer for those who feel like they're living different lives.

We all have different characteristics, but some of them dominate the others. So, even though you may have some characteristics of a D – Dominance, your overall personality profile may end up as an S – Steadiness.

Here's a breakdown of what the personalities mean.

•People with D (Dominance) personalities tend to be confident and emphasize accomplishing bottom-line results.

Characteristics:

•Direct

•Results-oriented

•Firm

•Strong-willed

•Forceful

•People with I (influence) personalities tend to be more open and emphasize relationships and influence or persuade others.

Characteristics:

•Outgoing

•Enthusiastic

•Optimistic

•High-spirited

•Lively

•People with S (Steadiness) personalities tend to be dependable and emphasize cooperation and sincerity.

Characteristics:

•Even-tempered

•Accommodating

•Patient

•Humble

•Tactful

•People with C (Conscientiousness) personalities tend to emphasize quality, accuracy, expertise, and competency.

Characteristics:

•Analytical

•Reserved

•Precise

•Private

•Systematic

If you were an employer, you would give your potential employees the DISC test to determine their personalities. Inevitably, you don't want someone with a High D personality in a support role; he or she won't be happy there. It'll be best to bring in someone with an S-dominant personality. The D personality would focus too much on completing the task – completing the mission – and could rub everyone else in the group the wrong way. Conversely, the S personality who emphasizes cooperation and sincerity will galvanize the team, making them a well-oiled machine that likes to work with one another.

Can you imagine how much more effective you would be as a sales rep, leader, manager, pastor, speaker, or even a parent if you could detect which personality group (D, I, S, or C) the person you are talking to is?

It would almost be as if you've been given an unfair advantage, given some private information, the inside scoop, the tea. Think of how much more influential you'd be in the Know, Like, and Trust psychology (we do business with people we feel we Know, Like, and can Trust) if you knew what to say to people depending on their personalities or traits.

For example, if you're a manager and someone wins an award, you'd know that the D and I would like a public display, an actual prize, and perhaps some time for an acceptance speech. However, the C and S person would be very uncomfortable in that situation, so maybe a company-wide email and a gift card for the winner would suit them better. If you force introverts in front of people to sing their praises, you'd embarrass them, not honor them. But how would you know if you didn't have them take the DISC test?

Every DISC style and personality are equally valuable, and everyone is a blend of all four styles. However, we are all defined by the dominating traits we possess. At the end of the day, we all want to be understood. Knowing oneself is Step 1. Take the DISC test and see if you are who you thought you were. Then, if you're in management, have your employees take one. There is usually a small fee for taking the test, however, since you purchased this book and I'm all about the return on investment of an organization working together in harmony and with everyone on the right seat of the bus, and for you to personally become a better sales rep is priceless.

I believe so much in this that I reached out to Dr. Michael Abelson and The Abelson Group, and am now certified with that group on the assessment test. As a result, I have an exclusive deal for you. Yes, you! Because you purchased this book and I'm certified with the group, you can go to www.FreedomDISCTest.com and take the assessment test for free! Please, I urge you to do it. You will understand yourself at a much deeper level. The secret to success and happiness is to truly know oneself and this is, in my opinion, the best way to do that.

KNOW OTHERS

Knowing how important it is to know yourself and others is great, except that if you don't know how to apply it to your business or relationships, it doesn't mean much. Let me show you different ways you can capitalize on knowing other people's personalities in tangible, real-world situations.

Imagine having the ability, a mini super-power, if you will, to understand others so well that you can determine the person's strengths, weaknesses, and major personality trait in one conversation.

If you've been in business long enough, you know that not every client is a good client. There are billions of people walking the planet, more than ever before; you may not want to work for all of them. If you've been an employer long enough, you also know that not every employee is good.

How much more effective would you and your company be if you could determine the right place for someone in your company by studying their reactions, answers, how they move, if they lean back and cross their arms or if they lean forward with their hands on the table, and how they communicate in an interview? Once you understand the DISC personalities and know the type of person you'd like to work for you, you'll have an unfair advantage in hiring a great candidate by using what's known as the Mirroring Technique.

The Mirroring Technique is just as it sounds, you do or "mirror back" what the person in front of you or is talking to you does. If you're in an in-person or video meeting and the person leans back, you lean back. If they lean forward, you lean forward. You also mirror how they talk, meaning if they speak firmly or fast, you do too; if they speak softly or slowly, you do too. The more the other person can feel at peace and comfortable with you, the better your chance of getting the deal or hiring them. If they see you act like them, subconsciously, they will feel like you are like them, which would give you the benefit of any doubt.

I have introduced people I hoped would work together, but because one of them didn't know how to read the other person, the deals didn't go through. One time I introduced my friend Jack to my friend Donny. Jack is a High D (Dominant), and Donny is a High C (Conscientiousness). Donny had to step out during the meeting and Jack looked at me with a huge smile. He told me how good he felt that he would do business with Donny and thanked me again for introducing them. Donny returned and the meeting concluded with Jack making the offer and Donny answered with, "Let me think about it."

I talked to Donny later and asked why he didn't do the deal. Donny said, "The deal sounded okay, but I'm unsure if Jack's the right person to do it with. His energy was a bit off for me."

"How so?" I asked.

"I know he's your friend, and I'm not saying he's a bad guy or anything, but he seemed a little domineering. I don't know if I want to go to meetings feeling my partner in this would try to bully me or not take me seriously. Also, speaking of seriously, he kept cracking jokes! Why would someone crack jokes during an important meeting with someone he doesn't know? I don't know how seriously he would take everything. No offense, but there's a better fit for me out there than him."

Jack didn't get the deal because he didn't use the Mirroring Technique. Donny is a very laid-back guy. His back didn't leave his chair the entire time; he went there with a folder, was taking notes, every hair was in place, and was extremely interested in specifics and analytics that supported Jack's claims, and spoke softly. In contrast, Jack was lively; he leaned forward the entire time, didn't take notes, laughed off the analytics as if it didn't matter, and kept turning the conversation to the results and how much money they would make. Had Jack mirrored Donny - sat back, taken notes, been prepared to speak on analytics, and not cracked jokes, he would have had the deal instead of the slow kiss of death called, Let me think about it – which means, *I'm too nice to say no to you in person, I'll tell you later via an email.*

I want to make this clear, the Mirroring Technique does not mean you change your personality or who you are. For example, if you're a New York sales rep and you're talking to a good ole country boy with a big Southern accent, don't start faking a Southern accent. This is the Mirroring Technique, not the Mimicking Technique. Don't start cussing if you never say cuss words and the person on the other end of the phone swears like a truck driver stuck in traffic. Stay true to who you are. Sales and relationships are rooted in authenticity. You stay being you. If you're that New Yorker, don't fake an accent, just slow down your speech and bring down your tone so the country boy doesn't think you're a city slicker. If you don't cuss and the truck driver does, tell him how much you hate being stuck in traffic also and bond over the experience. Experts mirror, amateurs mimic.

By understanding someone's personality traits and employing the Mirroring Technique, other people feel more comfortable going to the next step with you; whether it's a business deal, working for you, or a second date.

BENEFITS OF UTILIZING DISC RESULTS AND THE MIRRORING TECHNIQUE:

Your business will do much better if you know which salesperson or employee to interact with each client.

For example, let's say I own a small auto repair shop and someone comes in very frustrated and needs his car fixed yesterday. I'd immediately identify him as a high-D personality. If I called in Carl, a person with a High C personality, he'd frustrate the prospect. Carl would tell him what's wrong with the car, a few reasons why it may have happened, the parts he'll need to order, a range on how much they cost, and probably stop in mid-sentence and wonder out loud which brand the customer could use to save $3, and then tell him approximately how long it would take. That guy would never come to my shop again. However, if I brought another High-D mechanic, he'd just say, "Okay sir, this is what's wrong with the car, I'll have it done for you tomorrow at 10." Conversely, if a High C came in, wanting to know what we were going to do, why we were going to do it, and asking a bunch of questions, and I had my High D tell him the same thing, "Okay man, this is what's wrong with the car. I'll have it ready for you tomorrow at 10." That guy will never come to my shop again. Matching clients with the employees best suited to ease their fears is always a winning strategy.

Your business will do much better if you hire the right people for the right positions.

Let's say a very charismatic, high-spirited, and enthusiastic person came in to apply for the open accounting position. You'd know right away that it would most likely not work out. Yes, that person came to apply for the accounting position, but if you had the foresight to know that people that are High I's would be better in a sales capacity or working with other people instead of behind a desk working with numbers, as would appeal to a High C or High S, you could steer that person to a position the candidate is much better suited for and strengthen your company instead of weaken it because you liked the kid and hired him as an accountant, where he'd drive everyone in the department crazy.

To sum this chapter up:

Know thyself, who you are.

Know others, who they are.

Employ the Mirroring Technique.

Play big.

Be authentic.

BE UNSTOPPABLE

11

THE PERFECT AVATAR

THE AVATAR

There has been a lot of talk about avatars lately. First, let me explain the various meanings of it and then I'll quickly share why it's important for you to know your avatar.

The word, avatar, originates from Hinduism, it's explained as: *a manifestation of a deity or released soul in bodily form on earth; and incarnate divine teacher.* As technology advanced and video games became widely popular, another interpretation of the word, avatar, came about: *an icon or figure representing a particular person in video games, Internet forums, etc.*

Then, as if the word avatar wasn't getting convoluted enough, Film director, James Cameron, released an epic science fiction film, called Avatar. The actual avatar was the large, blue body of an alien (although it takes place in the alien's world, so to be more specific, I'll call him indigenous) and the alien (which in this case is a human being) who can't walk, can take over the blue body and control it, much like a parasitoid wasp; an insect that can control other insects.

However, there is another definition of the word, avatar, that deals in the business world, which is why I'm mentioning it – an avatar is made up of the characteristics, attributes, and finances of your ideal client. It could include geographic location, education level, title, age, sex (male or female), or physical disabilities.

In a previous chapter, I challenged you to discover your authentic _why_. Now, I want you to discover the perfect _who_.

So many people get into business and, immediately, their avatar is based on one criteria – the person with the most money, or, whoever can afford me. For example, if someone created a business that sold carbon steel pipes, their avatar would be a huge national company that builds bridges and skyscrapers across the world. It would be foolish to think otherwise, right? They got into business to make money and those companies can make them the most money.

In real estate, the instant avatar is the person who can buy the $35 million mansion on Biscayne Bay, Miami. However, they don't take into account that the person who could buy that mansion would want to work with someone much more experienced. Trust me, people that buy million dollar homes don't trust newbies. So, with the wrong avatar in a realtor's sites, the hungrier the realtor gets, until the realtor ultimately starves him or herself to death.

When I got into the real estate business, I only knew I needed to sell houses. Avatars weren't important to me. I sold a lot of houses but I didn't always relate to all of my clients, which led to missing out on many referrals I could have gotten. So, although I'd make a few thousand on a client, I would lose out on potentially tens of thousands of dollars more.

It's important for you to know your avatar; your ideal client. That's not to say that you'll only sell to clients that fit that mold, however, it will deepen the connection you have with those clients and, as a result, make more money on the back end through referrals than on the front end with the sale.

The good news is, you are a unique and diverse individual with many interests, so you can have multiple avatars.

For me, I enjoy working with military vets. I have spent nine years serving in the United States Marine Corps. I know their language because it's a part of my language. When I meet with a vet, there's an instant connection and trust developed that doesn't make sense with the short amount of time we've known each other. That's because we know what we've gone through and because of that, we have a brotherhood/sisterhood mentality. A vet would prefer to work with a vet.

My business started to explode once I focused more on working with vets. Had I known to hone in on veterans earlier, I could have been the #1 veteran real estate agent in the country. Working with like-minded individuals makes the work fluid and smooth.

Another avatar that I've found I worked extremely well with was first-time homebuyers. That being said, I've sold multi-million dollar homes, I've worked hard for it, and... what can I say, the commission is pretty nice. However I love the feeling of seeing someone or a couple buy their first home. Oftentimes, there are tears of happiness and warm embraces – it fuels my fire. I love handing people the keys to their first home. As someone who was willing to die for America while serving in the Marine Corps, it makes me feel great to help someone else achieve their American Dream.

These two avatars have much in common, although it may not look like it at first glance. The military gives great training on the duties they ask of you to perform, but finances and understanding how to get VA loans is not one of them. They don't teach you how to leverage your finances to become a homeowner, they're too busy teaching you to kill. Similarly, first-time home buyers don't have a clue as to how to position themselves for the best loans, schools teach math and English but not how to become a homeowner.

Another avatar that evolved organically during time is real estate agents. I started sharing what I knew to other realtors, then I started my brokerage and took it upon myself to coach realtors, and I've been massively successful. I will humbly say that I've coached many realtors who have become wealthy and successful. I'm proud of the track record I've established as a real estate coach. The more I was asked to speak at different events, I realized that growing a real estate business is very similar to the development of every other business. I went back to the drawing board and expanded my coaching criteria and curriculum. Now, we coach people from all over the country, whether they are marketers, plumbers, roofers, medium sized company's, or freelance writers – if they wanted to grow their business, we've been able to help.

WHO'S YOUR AVATAR?

But this is about you, dear reader. Who is your avatar? Once again, you'll find the correct answer inward and not by looking outward. What do you like to do? Where do you like to go? Do you like to cycle? Do you bike 3-4 times a week? Do you surf? Do you have a green thumb? What's your favorite sport? Do you play it? Not as a professional in MLB but are you in a softball league?

The answer I want you to get to is: who do you relate to? What type of person can you strike up a real conversation with due to the similar interests and insight you have on a particular subject? I'm not particularly big on watching sports but I love to work. I'd rather work than binge-watch on Netflix any day. It feeds my mind and my spirit, knowing I continue to move closer to my goals. When I communicate with others like me, it's at a high level. When you can naturally relate to someone, without forcing the conversation, doors open for everything else.

Understanding your avatar is a simple exercise. Not understanding your avatar will teach you painful lessons.

For example, if you are about to open a lollipop shop or cupcake shop and you find a good deal on a location, should you take it? The answer isn't as clear as one might think. What if the location was next to an LA Fitness? The person selling you the shop might make mention of the foot traffic you'd be exposed to, but if that foot traffic is made up of people who would most likely not buy your product, it's dead traffic. Would it not be smarter to open a health and supplement shop there? It's similar to opening a butcher shop specializing in pork in the middle of a Jewish or Muslim neighborhood, sure, there'll be plenty of people all around, but hardly any would be clients.

I KNOW I LIKE HER, BUT HOW DO I DATE HER?

Once you've identified your ideal clients, the next step is to attract them to you. Finding your avatar is a little different than finding a date, especially if you believe that line – opposites attract. In this case, opposites polarize and commonality attracts.

For example, let's say you're a conservative Christian, late night bars might not be where you'd find your avatars. However, there are many places where other Christians get together at least once a week. It may sound a little odd, but if you went to church a little more, not only would it do better for your mind, body, and soul, but also, the more other Christians know you, the better chance you've given yourself of helping them buy or sell their home. Use your social media to spread the good news – hey, Jesus Loves You and Let me bless you and help you buy your first home! As a veteran, I'm often at veteran events. I go to vet bars, local chapters, and I'm on veteran groups on Facebook.

Don't be phony. You can't relate to everyone. Accept that and focus on the ones you do relate to. I'm half-Puerto Rican and half Jewish, however, I don't canvas for clients at Orthodox Jewish Synagogues. I stand a much better chance attracting Veterans and first-time homebuyers.

There are online and in-person groups for whatever you like to do. Facebook has a group for just about anything, as does Twitter and Instagram, even LinkedIn if it relates to business. You can find in-person events on MeetUp.com. There are also conferences for everything from comics to science fiction to men who like to wear diapers.

I want to warn you though, getting your avatars attention isn't closing the deal. You still have to be interested in that person, ask the right questions, and make sure you are there to help. You are not trying to sell them, you are trying to attract them to you and your product.

Your avatar might evolve, and that's okay.

Your perfect customer today that can afford just $300,000 on a house might not work for you five years from now. With five more years of experience under your belt, your avatars probably fly in the $500,000 range, commensurate with your knowledge and experience level. I've had the privilege of selling many luxury properties, but I had to grow in experience and reputation in order for people of that ilk to trust me. Now, put me in a room with a high net worth individual and I easily have the right conversations that move the process forward. Remember, as you change and grow, so might your avatar. The important thing to know is who that avatar is at all times.

12

THE SWOT

DAVID VS. GOLIATH

If you've ever been in middle to upper management for a corporation, chances are, you've heard of the SWOT analysis. It is the go-to method to make sure you're doubling down on what you're good at, aware of what you're not good at, see the things you can benefit from in the future, and identify dangers to your company.

As you may be aware by now, I love to coach and teach people into success. However, in all honesty, this is one of my least favorite topics to teach. I find some of the content boring, but I teach it because it is very necessary to be successful in business. Also, I do this exercise periodically myself so that I'm not blindsided by anything. In this chapter, I'm going to break down what SWOT is, why you need it, and how it can help your business grow.

Whatever you do, don't be that proverbial "old guy" that is stuck in his ways and thinks things should be a certain way because it's always been like that. I'm here to tell you, if you're stuck in your ways, you'll die in your ways. Successful people understand shifts in their markets.

Companies that refuse to adapt and change don't just lose money, they become obsolete.

One of the more famous stories that prove that is the one between Blockbuster and Netflix. Blockbuster was the home-movie king. It was a national chain whose only rivals were small, independent video stores that, between you and me, mostly stayed in business because they were the only ones that sold X-rated videos.

Blockbuster was as dominant in their industry as there could be in a free enterprise market. They had locations all over the country, rights to the movies, happy repeat customers, and tons of money. They figured out correctly that people would be willing to pay less money and watch a movie at the comfort of their own home, equipped with the popcorn and candy sold at the theaters, which they could buy at their stores. Coincidentally, televisions, DVD players, and sound equipment also improved, which made it even easier for them to capitalize on the market. By 1994, Blockbuster had an $8.4 Billion evaluation.

Then in 1997, when Elton John ran away with the Billboard's with his hit, *Candle in the Wind,* and the original, *Men in Black* film dominated the Box Office, a little company named Netflix stepped quietly into the home-movie arena and offered an online subscription service through the Internet. Its sole advantage seemed to be that instead of going to the store, you could order the movies online. It worked because Netflix started to win market share.

However, the owners of Netflix reasoned that it would be better for them to partner with the giant Blockbuster and, as part of the deal, Netflix would run Blockbuster's online brand. Of course, that never happened, partly because Blockbuster laughed in Netflix's face. They didn't view Netflix as a threat and paid the ultimate price. In 2008, Netflix signed a deal with Starz to stream 1,000 movies and shows. In 2010, Netflix signed deals with Sony, Paramount, Lionsgate, and Disney' grabbing 20% of the market share of North American viewing traffic. In July of that same year, Blockbuster filed for bankruptcy. Should they have performed and adhered to an adequate SWOT analysis, the term would have been Blockbuster and chill instead of Netflix and chill. The question for you is, which brand do you want to be in this story, Blockbuster or Netflix?

SWOT ANALYSIS

SWOT stands for Strengths, Weaknesses, Opportunities, and Threats. If you don't know these four things about your business, and you figure them out, you've positioned yourself for growth. It's not just for big businesses, but for the solo-preneurs as well.

You need to understand that the market will shift, with or without your consent. Even things in your own company will change as new employees and technologies are brought in. In order to win today, flexibility is key. However, it's not so much on how far you can jump, it's more of where you should jump to.

The Marine Corps motto is, Semper Fidelis – Always Faithful. You don't have to serve in the Corps to know that. However, you may not have known that we in the Marines have another saying, Semper Gumbi – always flexible. We knew that we needed to be flexible as a military force at home and abroad due to the exterior events and policies continually shifting.

INTERNAL

The S – Strength and W – Weaknesses analysis is an internal evaluation. First, identify the strengths of your character/talents. What are you good at? Then examine the strengths of your company. What does your company do very well? What qualities separate you from your competitors? How do you stand out? Where do you have more customers, knowledge, or experience? What are the strengths of your employees? Do they love the company? Have you created a culture they could thrive in? Do you have systems that make it easy to work with you? What tangible assets do you have, such as intellectual property, capital, proprietary technology, etc.?

Once you've identified your strengths, go all in on them, double down. Put it in your marketing and branding. Let everyone know how good you are at the things you're very good at. There are professional basket-ball players that make millions of dollars but can't shoot to save their lives. Take Shaq, as an example, one of the greatest players of his day, yet one of the poorest free throw shooters. Shaq did work on his free throw, to no avail, but more importantly, he worked on his strength because that was his advantage. Some players, such as NBA legend, Dennis Rodman, became a multi-millionaire because of how well he rebounded – he rarely took shots! In today's NBA, people that are slow and can't dunk still make a great living because they developed a great three-point shot.

Finding out your weaknesses may not be as fun, as it will most likely hurt your ego, but it's just as necessary. Do you have limited capital? Do you not have a huge portfolio? Do you have resource limitations? Do you have personnel issues? Do an honest, internal assessment and find the holes in your offering or service. Where do you suck? What do you need help with? What does ABC Realty, ABC Cigar Shop, ABC Bicycle shop do much better than you?

Again, this only works if you're willing to be honest and not defensive. Once you know what your weaknesses are personally and as a company, you have the opportunity to change it. Here is where many small busi-ness owners and solo-preneurs go wrong. They identify their weaknesses and then, maybe because they are so talented in other areas, they take on the monumental task of doing something great that doesn't come natu-rally to them. It's foolish. It stunts growth. It makes people hate their jobs. This is what you do....

Take a blank sheet of paper and draw a line down the middle. Write down your strengths on one side and your weaknesses on the other. Make a plan on how you're going to let everyone know about your strengths and execute that plan. As for the weaknesses, write it up in a Job Offer Form and put out an ad for someone with those skills to come in and plug those holes. If you see someone happy and successful, that's because they figured out what their weaknesses were and had the right person turn those weaknesses into strengths. If you do the Strengths and Weaknesses analysis, you'll become stronger and less weak. Makes sense, right?

EXTERNAL

The O – Opportunities and T – Threats are external. These are things outside of your control, but you need to be aware of them before you miss out on opportunities or you get blindsided by change.

Opportunities only exist when you know of them.

If you never knew about something, it was never a reality in your universe. When trying to capitalize on opportunities, you need to do your research. One of the biggest mistakes storefronts and restaurants fail is that they fall in love with something that doesn't produce revenue, such as the view or the interior design, or the amount of space. Those that don't take into account the competition and the commute for their ideal customers will soon find themselves wishing they had another location.

Find your passion and find a way to make money on it is what many "gurus" are saying today. For one, they're saying it because they're pandering to a generation of people who want to do just that. While it could be the right call for some, not everyone is going to be successful doing what they love. Not everyone may love what you do. Or, even if people do love it as much as you, they may not pay for your consultation, service, or product.

I find that many markets in real estate are still underserved. It's surprising because it seems as if everyone and their mother is a realtor. If I were to start all over again, I'd find an area where there is no dominant realtor or brokerage; a zone where you don't see signs of him or her, and I'd open up a shop there. I'd put ads on buses that drive through there, benches, send out mailers, knock on doors, and fill that place up with my name and face.

America is still the land of opportunity, but you have to identify it. Ask yourself, what underserved markets are there near me? Where can I get free press/media coverage for my company or me? Which companies are going out of business that I can buy things for pennies on the dollar?

The next thing to do is to identify the threats or you will share Blockbuster's fate. But this is the caveat to this one; I don't want you to focus on them, I want you to understand them so that you can focus on the opportunity that may come with it. When analyzing threats, I recommend taking a holistic approach. If someone is opening up a lollipop shop next to yours, you may want to consider offering other candies that the new one won't provide.

If you're in the real estate field, you may view inventory decrease or increase as a threat and it may be the case, but then again, they both create price shifts, one up and one down. Depending on how it goes, you can capitalize and put all of your attention on the avatars that it would benefit.

News happenings, global events, and pandemics can negatively or positively impact a market. Fake news can affect your business as well. I spoke with a coaching client of mine who is a realtor recently who complained that she had a serious, engaged buyer but when she gave him a call, the man said he's going to wait to see what happens with the reported rash of Monkey Pox – Monkey Pox!

When you do a threat analysis, try not to do it from a scarcity or fearful mindset. I don't concern myself with whether a cup is half full or half empty, whenever I'm thirsty I just drink the water and put more in. There are answers to every question, and sometimes the biggest opportunities come wrapped around a problem.

I have been a broker for many years. I grew my company to having three offices. We were an award-winning brokerage and were even nominated by Inman Magazine as the Most Innovative. We were having fun and making money. So, when the opportunity to move to another brokerage knocked on my door, I ignored it for the first 18 months.

I was doing just fine... like Blockbuster. I had a 90%-10% split with my realtors. If one of my realtors earned a $6,000 commission, the company would get $600. With the collective 10%, we paid the three rental spaces, maintenance, electricity, staff, printers, taxes, water, etc. My break-even number was at around $60,000 a month, and that was before I paid my own mortgage, cars, food, gas, clothing, etc. Still, we were profitable enough that I saw little startup Netflix, err, I mean, a new startup real estate company but didn't pay much attention to it.

However, as I continued to travel across the country to speak and coach, I started seeing more realtors join that firm. It was as if they didn't exist one day to coming out of the woodwork the next. I finally sat down with someone who had a similar sized business to mine that joined this company. She told me that the main reason why she gave up her own brokerage was because this new company allowed her to release the stresses of owning a brokerage, which are substantial. Then she broke down why a realtor would want to leave a traditional brokerage and join little Netflix, umm, this new real estate company.

As a former military man and someone who loves history, I am convinced that those who don't know history are doomed to repeat it. So, I spoke with my wife and team at length. If you remember correctly, early on in this book I shared that my main mission in life is to have freedom. While I don't presume to think that there is a one-size-fits-all in any business, meaning that for some people this new company won't make sense for them, it made sense for me. I formed The Freedom Organization, and I have not regretted it for a second. I get to do more of my passion; recruiting, training, selling, and coaching. I also get to travel to speak on more stages, write books, and utilize my other strengths, all of which make me a much happier person, husband, father, boss, and friend.

My hope to you, dear reader, as you read this is that you put the things I teach here into practice. Make some time, either by yourself, with your executive team, or your entire staff, and do the SWOT Analysis. If you do it honestly and implement what you need to, you may become more successful, and maybe a lot happier along the way.

13

LEADS, LEVERAGE, & SALES TECHNIQUES

LEADS

It doesn't matter your business; you won't have it for long if you don't sell.

Sales, then, is the lifeblood of any business. To say it differently, clients are the lifeblood of any business. However, before someone becomes a client, they must be a prospect. If you can't find prospects, you can't have clients. Another term for a prospect is a lead. The definition of a lead for a business is – a potential consumer who is interested in what your company offers.

If sales is the lifeblood of every business, a lead is its heart, from where the blood flows.

It doesn't matter what you're selling: pool installations, bicycles, ice cream, homes, lollipops, cake designs, plumbing, etc. Business 101 will tell you that every business needs to find leads and convert them into clients. I'm talking to you. You can wing it and pray for God to open the windows of heaven to bring you clients miraculously, you can go the beach, spread your arms, say manifestations and vibrate with the universe to get you clients, OR you can learn how to get leads and convert them to clients. I wonder which one Harvard Business School would recommend.

As of this writing, my daughters, Elizabeth and Allison are 15 and 13, respectively. They have heard my spiel many times. They have also, to the delight of my wife and I, figured out the career path they want to take. Color me shocked when neither one of them wanted to be an entrepreneur. Ellie wants to be a dermatologist and Allie an anesthesiologist. During a family dinner, after hearing me say that every business needs a lead, Allie said, "Abba, I get what you're saying, but why would *we* (her sister and her) need to know how to get leads if we're going to be doctors?" Ellie nodded her head in agreement.

"Good point," I conceded, smiling. "But that's not to say no one is getting leads for the doctors. In your cases, the hospitals will be advertising to the community to bring in the business that would substantiate the salary you get. But should either or both of you want to start your own practice, there will not be any help from the hospital to find you the people who need your service."

To you, dear reader, if you don't have a multi-million-dollar-a-year entity generating leads for you, as a hospital does for doctors and its staff, break out a pen and a notebook because I'm going to teach you five basic ways on how to get leads in today's economy. There is so much more that goes with this, but I'll touch on these five for the sake of not having an encyclopedia-sized book.

#1 Content Creation

Creating content is one of the best free ways to get people to pay attention to who you are and what you do. If you consistently put out organic content that people consume consistently, they will feel like they know you, trust you, and maybe even like you if you were ever to meet.

When I'm having interactive conversations from a stage, one of the questions I always get is – "How many Facebook posts do I need?"

My friend, the answer isn't a number to the number of Facebook posts. If you want to grow a following and scale a business, you need to ask better questions. A better question would be, "David, how should I display my content in a way that will be the most effective, least costly, and provide the maximum return on my time and money?"

Here's the answer – jot this down.

Facebook is not the end-all-be-all anymore. But while I'm on Facebook, let me share the different ways you can use it to market your offering. You can do Facebook Posts, Stories, and Reels. You can then take that same piece of content, or those same pieces of content, and put it on Instagram in the form of a post, story, or reel. If your content is of video, you can take that same content and post it on YouTube or put it on their Shorts. That same content can also be put on X, formerly known as Twitter, and post it there and start conversations. Then, put that same content on LinkedIn and tag some people interested in reading it, even if they're in the same field, because you want engagement.

The more engagement (likes, shares or comments), the more the platform's algorithms put your content in front of more people. Then, you can put the content on TikTok. Yes, TikTok. I can't tell you how many times I've purchased something for my daughters by what they saw on TikTok. Although there is some crossover, each platform reaches different demographics. The more engagement (likes, shares, or comments) your content generates, the platform's algorithms put it in front of more people.

Another question I get is, "What type of content should I create?" Again, to not make this book super long, I'll answer with one way, although in my coaching program, I break down the many different forms of content that work. For now, let's consider podcasting.

Let's say I video-record a 20-minute podcast. I would upload it to many podcast platforms such as Lybsin, Anchor, Apple, Spotify, Captivate, Buzzsprout, etc. This is what 97% (my opinion, it could be higher) of podcasters do. But you're reading this book to be better than 97% of your competition, so you should do this: Take the video and cut up short, 7-13 second clips, and also longer videos. Write down quotes from what was said, go to Canva.com, and create post-able content in the form of great-looking posts, flyers, cards, etc. I teach my coaching students to extrapolate 47 pieces of content from one 20-minute podcast!

Let's take this a little further. You do one podcast a week, of which you get 47 pieces of content. A few times a week, you also upload things you do in your day-to-day life: running, working out at the gym, going to the movies with your kids, playing tennis, going to a game, or the amazing Chicken Milano and Empanadas you just made. Trust me, people love that stuff. Just as much as they want to know you're credible at what you do, they also want to know you're a genuine and relatable person.

Now you have 40-50 pieces of content plus 12 more a week, giving you 50+ ways people can consume your message and brand. Doing this would yield 250+ pieces of monthly content generated from just four podcasts!

When I say that, some people's eyes light up. "Holy crap! Even if I do a quarter of that, it could change my business!" Other people's shoulders slump, "Holy crap. I don't have the skills or the bandwidth to do all of that!" I say to those people, "Don't worry, you don't have to do all the work. Just create the original content, and I can show you how to leverage it, which I'll show you, dear reader, later in this chapter.

#2 Paid Ads

If someone asks me to do something, I might do it. However, I'd definitely do it if someone paid me. Facebook, Instagram and other social media sites are the same. They'll put up your content in front of some of your 'friends' for free. But if you paid them, they'd put your content in front of many more 'friends' and people who fit the criteria you are looking for.

Paid content works better than non-paid content, just like a billboard will get you more noticed than not having a billboard. However, a billboard from a no-name will bear little fruit. But if you were to post 253 pieces of content across many platforms six months before you put up your billboard, it will have a much better chance of getting you recognized by someone other than your mother. I know many business owners who would not have become nearly as successful if it weren't for paid ads.

#3 Referrals

I also know many business owners who don't use paid ads because they have a staunch referral network. They don't pay for marketing outside of business cards, websites, hosting, etc., because so many people know them, like them, and trust them enough to refer their friends and family.

A referral is like a cheat code for converting a lead into a client. Let's go through a scenario: your friend Mike introduces you to his pool guy, Bill. Both of you know and like Mike. Mike introduced you to Bill because he does a good job cleaning his pool, and, just as importantly, he knows how much Bill charges. He also knows you can afford what Bill charges. So, right off the bat, you have a qualified lead - someone who needs your service and can afford it.

Because both of you know Mike, you both want the deal to work. If you're the type that usually gets a few quotes before making a decision, because of your friendship with Mike, you most likely won't get another quote, eliminating any potential competition from Bill to close you as a client. That's like cheating!

For the life of me, I'll never understand why entrepreneurs don't ask their clients, friends, and family members for referrals.

Write this down so you remember it: a referral is the easiest lead to close. You do have to work it though. Consistently thank those who give you referrals and continue to let them know you depend on them.

#4 Affiliates

An affiliate is a person who promotes on our behalf with the agreement that whoever they bring that you close, they will get a piece of the pie. It's just like paying a commission-only salesperson. They only get paid when you get paid. However, unlike a commission-only salesperson, they don't work for you. Through a designated link or some other form to track their leads, they know how much money to expect, commensurate with how much business they brought you.

I know people, particularly some with huge followings, who practically live off affiliate agreements. I, too, offer affiliate agreements. When someone brings a student to my coaching program, they get 20% of what we charge while helping their friend get the needed knowledge to grow their business. It's the elusive triple win: they get paid, I get a new student I would otherwise not be able to help, and their friend gets the help they need! Win-Win-Win.

Do this; write down a list of everyone you know that has proximity to your ideal clients. Come up with a way to track the referrals they send you and agree with a kickback (please make sure it's legal in your type of business) or percentage of what they would make for each deal. Take your time and create that list, then execute it and start getting leads from people who would have never even known you. That, my friend, is the power of affiliates.

#5 Cold Calls

Most people think cold calling is outdated. They shudder at the thought of making 70 phone calls to get 20 people on the phone and get a no from every 60 people they talk to before getting a yes. I get it. However, that doesn't mean cold calls aren't a great way to get leads and turn them into clients.

Some of the smarter, and, subsequently, more successful entrepreneurs hire call centers to do outbound calls. They could be out showing a lakefront property, playing golf, or reading a great book called The Truth About Failure, while people in their radius are receiving phone calls on their behalf. Sure, there are legalities and Do Not Call lists, but in no way does that limit or erase what 60, 200, or 500 calls a day can do.

LEVERAGE

The content you produce, just like the cold calls a call center makes on your behalf, doesn't have to be 100% on you to deliver. If you wanted to produce 250+ pieces of content a month, you don't have to slump your shoulders and say, "Holy crap. I don't have the skills or the bandwidth to do all of that!" Leverage it.

If you're a doctor, you are most valued in front of a patient. If you're a business owner, you're most valued closing big deals and creating partnerships that would ensure the longevity of the business. If you're worth $300 an hour, don't do the work you could pay someone $12 an hour to do!

Let's talk basic math – if you make a clean $100,000 a year, you earn $48.08 per hour. If you can pay someone $12 an hour for five hours a week, you'd be paying $60 per week. If you did the job, it would take you twice as long because it's not your specialty, not to mention it wouldn't come out twice as good. You would have spent $576 worth of your time when you could have gotten better results and only paid $60 if you hired a professional editor. That editor could have fixed or cleaned any audio issues, cut and sliced up the content to your specifications, and put them on the social media platforms you want to be on while you close deals or service clients. If you're a coach who charges $200, $300, or more an hour, what the hell are you doing creating all these pieces of content? No bueno! Leverage it out!

In other words, I'm sorry if this comes across as harsh, but it's essential you to pick up what I'm laying down here – no one goes into McDonald's, puts on an apron and a hat, and flips their own burgers. Time is money, no matter how you look at it. If you hire an editor to help with your content, you're making money, if you don't, you're losing it. Stop mowing your own lawn and spend that time making money or creating memories with your family.

The first hire for a doctor starting a practice should be an assistant. Imagine if the doctor hires a massage therapist first. Who would take and make calls, set the appointments, and greet the new patients when they enter? Similarly, the first hire an entrepreneur, especially a real estate professional, should make is an assistant. Second? An accountant. But that's a topic for my coaching program. There's a process for selecting the right person, some of which I covered in Chapter 10 when

I taught on the DISC assessment test. I can help you ensure you get the right person if you need me to.

Leveraging means doing what you're best at and letting someone else create invoices, confirm appointments, send receipts, edit your content, upload the content on various platforms, qualify leads, and do necessary administrative tasks. Can you imagine how much more productive and happy you'd be if freed from Email Jail? That would entail having someone check your work emails, filter them, write the responses for you, send the outgoing ones out for your approval, and put all you need to know about the other ones in one email. I hope you're getting this. I'm giving you fire right now!

Leveraging also means scaling. Imagine being a doctor with a practice that can't take on any more clients. You could be content—comfortable even. However, you could leverage your overflow patients and bring in another doctor if you wanted to scale. The same goes for being a successful but too-busy of a realtor. You could bring in an agent and offer a 50/50 split from the clients you provide. This way, your bank account grows without your time being consumed even more.

Leveraging also comes into play with the referrals, as mentioned earlier. Go from being your only salesperson to having 100 people selling for you, giving the leads to your assistant, to just closing deal after deal. If it were me, I'd rather be closing deals during the day and toasting my wins at night instead of being my own administrator who, once again, is slacking because I'm too busy doing other things.

Too many think an assistant, editor, social media manager, or paying for any assistance is too expensive. Do the math yourself on what you're making and how much you'd pay out. How much more could you make, and how much would it improve your quality of life if you didn't have to do work you hate doing but needs to be done and, instead, do what you love and are great at?

Leverage and grow. Don't and plateau. Leverage is a requirement for scaling a business!

SALES TECHNIQUES

A sale has three undeniable stages: before, during, and after. No matter what you're selling, each of your leads or clients is somewhere on that scale. By the way, you're always selling. Whether it's your product or service, convincing your spouse and kids to see the movie you want to see, on a second date hoping for a third, trying to talk an officer out of getting you a speeding ticket, or convincing your best friend to leave that crazy ex alone. In almost every human interaction, there is some transaction in the balance. But, regarding sales for your business, you should always be selling, even when you're in the fulfillment stage.

Before I dive into any particular technique, know that there are 100s of them. There are many different approaches and sales philosophies, far too many to cover them right here. The truth is, you only need to understand a handful of them. Once you find them, be consistent, tweaking them to your personality and experience. Over time, you will get better and better at it. The important thing is to continue to study them and hone your skills with them. I'm not going to get into closing, assuming, utilizing urgency, handling objections, or the myriad of different ways to close someone. Instead, I will be very practical here, teaching a simple and proven way to move a lead along the sales cycle.

I assume you have some online presence – a website or social media page, for example. What do you do when someone clicks on an ad, sends you a DM from your business Facebook page, or clicks through a Google search and goes to your website? Do you have a system in place to ensure that the person is touched and followed up with? Most people don't.

I'm going to keep this simple because it is. When someone reaches out, you should have a pre-written email automatically generated and sent to the person. The email's message should be your mission with any other lead – try to get in front of that person, whether online or in person. Sure, take a phone call, but only as a last measure. Video conferencing is much more relatable than a phone call, not to mention you can share your screen to show the lead what you'd like them to see. Nothing, and I mean nothing, beats meeting someone in person. They are serious about whatever you offer if they're willing to take time out of their day to meet you.

So your emails or first phone call should end something like this:

You: When do you want to meet?

Lead: I don't know. I'm not sure it's for me.

You: Maybe it is, maybe it isn't. When do you want to meet to find out?

Lead: How much would this cost me?

You: That varies on what suits you best. Either way, the cost is insignificant if it works, right? Would you like to meet on Tuesday at one or Wednesday at three?

Here are five essential things to do to help you close more sales.

1. Build Rapport. Sales techniques rarely work if you don't build rapport with the lead. There are many ways to do that, but that's not the purpose of this chapter. If a car salesperson doesn't build rapport with a lead, that person might very well get the same car from another company because they didn't like that salesperson. Be personable, be on time, be inquisitive, be prepared, and you can build honest rapport.
2. Ask for the sale. Don't ever leave a meeting without asking for the sale. Even if you have to come back with answers to questions you didn't know, get a commitment that should you come back with a satisfactory response, the person will sign with you. Every meeting is an opportunity to close.
3. Offer an incentive. If the sale isn't coming to fruition, offer a deal. Offer a discount. Throw in a freebie. People love perks. Some people buy their cars from a particular dealer because the oil changes are free. Do an inventory of what else you can offer that would still make the deal suitable for you.
4. Create Urgency. Tell the prospect the offer is only available until Friday at the close of business. Tell the listeners of your podcast that you only have 100 left. I've seen people in podcast use urgency brilliantly, stating they can only assist 50 people

when I knew damn well they could service 30,000. The truth about people is that no one likes to miss out on a great opportunity. Mix the incentive with urgency and it will get more people to take your offer.

5. Create Remorse. It's okay not to be super optimistic all the time. Meaning, ask tough questions.

"What would happen if you don't do this?"

"Do you think you will reach your goals quicker without my product?"

"How much time have you already put into this?"

Too many people lose out on deals because they only talk about the product or service's benefits rather than the ramifications of not having it.

In closing this chapter, know that if you correctly handle the lead throughout the three stages – before, during, and after the sale, most consumers will be repeat customers and potentially referral sources.

14

A MOMENT OF CLARITY

I want to congratulate you for going this far into the book. If nothing else, it shows a willingness to improve your quality of life by improving your business. However, I also want to be direct with you. I am, after all, a coach. Respectfully, chances are that this is not the first book of this genre you've purchased. You've also most likely attended seminars, been coached, sat in on webinars, or paid for online courses to shorten the road to your goals. The reason why you're reading this book could very well be because you didn't implement what was already taught to you.

Life is short. If you know you're not going to implement the teachings here that have helped business owners across the country, do someone else a favor and gift them this book. It's not meant to be a good read and for people to pat me on the back and tell me how much they enjoyed it; it's designed to be a road map for people to follow to get to their destinations as efficiently and effectively as possible.

Take a moment to visualize where you would have been if you had opted for the coaching or implemented the tactics and techniques you've learned over the years. Know that you can't change the past but that you can start creating new habits today.

I hope this clarity also makes you re-commit to yourself and your future.

Decide that you will take action on what you've gleaned from this book.

If you do, I can't wait for you to turn the page because I put everything together in the following chapter. I call it - The Foundation.

If you utilize this book as intended, you could be the next person to hold their book on stages across the country. If you're committed, turn the page.

15

THE FOUNDATION

I've shared real-world, real-life, practical, and applicable examples to help anyone grow their business, regardless of where it is. I've used my own stories, other people's stories, and even famous people to help you mitigate any ~~failures~~, I mean, hiccups you may encounter down the road. If your business is in the infancy stage, use it to become an average company. If it's average, use it to be above average. If it's above average, use it to become excellent. If it's excellent, use it to dominate your industry.

I designed this book so you can return to it in different growth spurts of your professional life and it will continue to provide value. In the event that things take a downturn, use it as an emergency lifeline. Just as when there's a raging fire, to get to a hose or ax, break the glass (open the book) and use the essential teaching to put the fire out. Above all, remember this – failure is not an option; it shouldn't even be in your vocabulary. Every time that nagging, worried voice confuses you and fills you with fear or doubt, use it not just to mute it but to vanquish it from ever coming back. I'm going to attempt, as best I can, to put the most important things you need to know in this chapter. I've already mentioned these things, but for someone to remember and take action, it's best when things are repeated or reinforced.

You're not entitled to success. No one is. Success is not a right of passage. It doesn't get handed down from generation to generation. Success must be earned, worked for; sometimes fought and bled for. The three fundamentals on being successful are:

1. Never quit.
2. Take action.
3. Failure is not an option.

Success is your duty, obligation, and responsibility.

Don't depend on Statistics. Some people use them as truths or absolutes. They're not. It should mean nothing to you if 71% of people from your neighborhood don't go to college. That stat has nothing to do with you, the way you think, your goals, or the vision you created for your future. You create your stat about your life. If it's college, it will either be 100% or 0%; you went or you didn't. Please don't give a second thought to Forbes' claim that more than 80% of businesses don't make it five years. You create the stat about your business. Whatever you do, don't rely on statistics to help you out. You may like a statistic that claims you have a 95% chance to win big – it might make you a little lazy or over-confident.

Tell time what to do. Manage your time and you'll manage your success. Focus your time on the most valuable things you can be doing first and always. Time Valuement.

Work – Life – Balance. There's no such thing as an equal amount of time spent on each. Financial success may require spending more time at work, while home-life success is ensuring your time at home is quality time. You don't need to spend 50% of your time on each. Find what works for you and your spouse/partner and children. Share your vision for your family and get them on the same page and you'll achieve the work-life-balance that works for you and your family.

There is no one-size-fits-all for how successful entrepreneurs balance their work and home life.

<u>Mindset.</u> You need to train your mind on how it acts and reacts to internal and external situations. Building a foundational way of thinking is essential to get you past the roadblocks you and your business will undoubtedly encounter. Your thoughts are foundational to creating your business' success. If you build a straw house on sand, the simplest rain can ruin it. However, suppose you construct a massive steel building capable of withstanding category five hurricanes and doors and lay the foundation deep into good soil. In that case, nothing will knock it down, regardless of whatever storm may come your way. Sure, it might get dinged, the paint might chip off, a car may have been flipped and smashed into a door, but the building will remain standing. The debilitating thoughts are the storms; despair, fear, scarcity, hopelessness, loneliness, pride, arrogance, and the like. Continue to train your brain and become storm-proof!

<u>The Hero Code.</u> How you handle situations defines who you are as a human being. The responses you give to actions are your reactions. Become the hero in your own story by exhibiting the following characteristics:

Have courage. Enter the cave, regardless of how dark it looks.

Be humble. It's better for others to brag about you than you brag about yourself.

Don't be too proud to ask for help.

Don't be afraid to sacrifice for what you want – success often requires sacrifice.

Have integrity – keep your word at all costs.

Persevere – don't quit.

It is your duty to do the job you get paid to do.

Find a way to forgive and you'll live a happier life.

If you can put these all together, you'll be unstoppable in business, at home, in your community, for your family, and future generations.

Innovate or stagnate. Continually feed your mind with new, better ways of doing what you do. Have conversations with people who will stimulate ideas and who can see barriers you can't see at the moment. One of your core responsibilities is to innovate at a high level. If you study your competition just to beat them, you probably never will. Learn from them! Emulate them. And then, once you can do what they're doing, improve and innovate on what you learned. That's how to beat them.

Standard Operating Procedures. You'll only grow through luck if you don't write down SOPs. This is what transforms a small business into a corporation, an entrepreneur into a business owner. If you're a solopreneur, how can you grow if you don't have something or a system in place for someone to take over your duties or the duties you don't like or could be better at? If/when you have a changeover in employees, the SOP will allow the business to not lose momentum.

Understand your why. This may look easy, but it's one of the deepest, brutal introspective-thinking a person can do. Be honest with yourself. Do you want to be rich? Own it. Do you want to be the best at what you do? Own it. Do you want people to respect you? Own it. As I mentioned in chapter eight, I had to hire a coach to help me get through all the bullshit about who I thought I wanted to be and disregard what others thought I should be. I found my way and it has liberated me.

Freedom is my why. It's what motivates me to get out of bed at five a.m. It compels me to push through and be at the gym at 5:30. This might come across as egotistical to you, but with the utmost respect, I can't care. It's not that I don't care, it's that my future is on the line and I can't care. I must stay true to why I feel I'm on this planet.

I want the freedom to travel with my family and friends without losing out on opportunities or income. Freedom is fought for. Freedom is died for. Dig through the fake humility, stop worrying about what others might think about you, and be totally honest about your goals and desires.

Take the journey and find your real why. It'll be the fuel that will

**power you through long stretches of sand and desert –
disappointments and hiccups.**

The 5-3-1. Stop dreaming and start goal-setting like a pro. Write down how your life will look in five years, three years, and one year. Come to an agreement with yourself on where you want to be in one, three, and five years, and then reverse engineer the way to get there. No matter where you are in your career or how big or small you are, this is something that should be done consistently. It helps pave the way for you to reach your goals.

Get to know your money. What's it doing for you? Take an inventory of how much comes in and how much goes out. Find out if your spending is necessary or if you lack self-discipline. Audit yourself. Do an open and honest financial affidavit on your money and learn how to make money do more for you than it is now.

Know thyself. I hope you do the written exercise and find your authentic why. However, that's different than knowing yourself. What are your strengths and weaknesses? Take advantage of personality tests such as the DISC Assessment Test. You might hate your job, regardless if it pays well because what you do is not compatible with your personality. In the resource page of this book there will be a link where you can take your profile disc test for free!

Know others. Utilize the knowledge of the DISC test to ensure that you align with the right people to join your company. It doesn't matter if you have a full bus; what matters is that every person is in the right seat on the bus.

**Take the time and learn the incredibly valuable art of reading
people so that you can put them in positions to succeed and
where they'd be most happy and effective.**

The Mirroring Technique. We do business with people we feel we know, like, and can trust. The truth is, we like people like ourselves. You gain an advantage if you leverage the mirroring technique and make people feel comfortable with you. Utilize your knowledge of personalities to adjust accordingly and get the sale!

Who's your avatar? You might think anyone breathing is a prospect, but that's not necessarily true. Sure, you may be able to service many different people, but who is your ideal client? How much money do they make? How responsive are they to your questions? Gather up Intel for your perfect client. Then and only then can you create a campaign to work with more people like that. Imagine how much happier and more productive you would be if all of your clients could afford your services easily, valued your opinion, gave you referrals, and were repeat customers. First, you need to identify who that avatar is.

SWOT. Not all aspects of business are exciting. To me, SWOT defines this. However, it's a necessary tool to sustain or grow a business. SWOT stands for Strengths, Weaknesses, Opportunities, and Threats. Remember that the focus on Strengths and Weaknesses are *internal* and Opportunities and Threats are *external* in this evaluation. Do an internal evaluation of these four major components of your business. Start spending more time on your strengths, and farm out your weaknesses (an employee or subcontract). Put together a plan to capitalize on your opportunities. Please don't make it up as you go along every single time. What are you, nuts? Find the model that works and get in a groove, continue to do it, and then get in your zone. Study your market and find upcoming threats. There could be changes in technology, laws, or climate change. Prepare for them so that when that tsunami lands, your house will not get washed away.

Leads. You only have a business if you have customers and only have customers if they are leads first. As technology continues to be a more significant part of our professional lives, you must leverage various free and paid tools to reach the widest audience possible. There are many ways to do that, but, in this book, I've laid out five sure-fire ways so that you don't have to tinker and waste time or money. Create original content and distribute them across all social media platforms. Pay for social media ads to get a wider audience from your avatars. Don't stop asking your friends, family, and clients for referrals; it's a cheat code to success. Develop relationships with affiliates; influencers who can bring you business for a percentage of the sale or a referral fee. Don't sleep on cold calls, it's still a very effective way to find qualified leads. If you're too busy to make them, hire a call center to do them for you. Imagine what your business would look like if you had 5, 10, or 15 more appointments a week that you spent no time getting!

Leverage. Continue to do and get better at what you are best at and hire others to do what you don't like or are not good at. This will increase your quality of life and make you much more productive. Do the math on how much you earn per hour or week and figure out how much it would cost to hire someone, even if it's part-time. You'll find you can afford an assistant, video editor, salesperson, or call center.

Leverage your time and the money you make by hiring others and double, triple, or quadruple your effectiveness!

Sales Techniques. There are a plethora of sales techniques and there was no way we could put them all in this book or that you would remember them all. However, if you do these five things well, even if you consider yourself shy or an introvert, you'll be successful at closing deals.

1. Build a rapport with the person you're meeting with.
2. Make sure to ask for the sale before leaving the meeting.
3. If you don't get the deal initially, offer an incentive.
4. If the prospect is thinking about it but has yet to decide, create urgency by telling them the offer is available for a limited time.
5. If it looks like you won't get the sale, create remorse.

Let the client tell you what would happen if they don't use your product or service. After all, they're talking to you because they have a pressing need. If you can do these things, you can sell.

Remember, my friend, luck is fickle.

You can't depend on it to become successful. The best athletes, celebrities, and business professionals all have coaches. Allow this book to coach you to grow in areas required in order to live a happy and successful business career. Also, consider joining the Freedom Achiever Academy and allow me the honor of personally coaching you to success, wealth, and happiness. Turn the page to find out how!

16

GOAL SET AND TAKE ACTION

IT'S TIME TO IMPLEMENT

Congratulations, dear reader, for getting to the end of this book, which has taken decades of experience and hundreds of millions of dollars in sales to put together. You reached two of my many goals for writing it: 1 – that you purchase it, and 2 – that you absorb the information that can catapult your business into the next stratosphere. However, my third goal is most important – 3 – that you apply what I've taught here. If you do nothing with any knowledge, that knowledge is worse than useless; it's an anchor weighing in your brain, sapping positive energy from you because you know you should be doing something valuable but aren't.

If it's okay with you, I want to end our time together by putting my heart in my hand. My goal is to impact the lives and businesses of more than a million people. I've put my heart and soul into putting this book together over the last three years. I've written, studied, rewritten, I've had partners betray me and make me wonder if I was doing the right thing, I've had lawsuits come up against me and put me near the point of desperation – but I've never quit, meaning; I haven't failed.

Justice was served in the end, and I walked out of the valley of the shadow of death with more certainty that this book is precisely what billions of business owners need to get through the tough times, step out of the storm, and walk into a beautiful, sunlit morning.

I'd consider it an honor and privilege if you let me know your thoughts on this book. I am about to give you my personal Instagram account so you can give me your direct feedback. I'd love to know that I either reiterated something you knew you should have been doing but have been putting off or that you learned something new – maybe the DISC Personality Tests or S.O.P.s – and have implemented them. I dream of waking up to hundreds of messages that would take me the entire day to read and answer. That, my friend, is good living!

Utilizing the knowledge in these pages will give you the power to change the game for you and your business. It will open new doors for you, eliminate the crabs that try to keep you in the hole, and help you soar with eagles.

I believe a new season is upon you, but it makes no difference if I'm the only one - you must believe it! It's time to implement.

YOUR BEST LIFE

Take one moment, right here, right now, and imagine what your life would look like if you implemented the teachings of this book. Imagine if you finally let go of some 'friends' holding you back and got into a new circle of people who, like you, are out to slay dragons and make their mark on this world. Imagine having a system in writing on how your company operates. Imagine leveraging Time Valuement - telling time what to do and ensuring you do the day's most important tasks first. Imagine living up to the Hero Code. Imagine writing down your 5-3 1 goals and the actionable steps to attain them and then actually start doing them. Imagine understanding who your perfect avatar is and putting together a plan to attract those types of people. Imagine leveraging other people's talents and hiring an assistant or call center to help you maximize your reach while doing the things you are great at.

Imagine coming to terms with your true self and understanding your real – why. What would your life look like in 12 months if you went full force with experienced knowledge and proven methodologies supporting your every effort? Imagine having a fresh sense of tenacity to ensure failure doesn't come close to your career.

What would your life look like in 12 months? What vacation would you be planning for your family? What home or investment property would you be looking to purchase? What car would you test drive, knowing that in a few short months you can finally buy it? How many short-term rentals do you own? What Christmas present will you get your assistant that's become so valuable to you and your business? Is your perfect lollipop now sold in stores across the country? Are you much more respected by your spouse, kids, extended family, friends, and community? How does that feel?

Allow me to share one of my goals. I write my 5, 3, and 1-year goals often. They change at times, but because I am in tune with what I want; my why – Freedom – and I'm not ashamed to go after my heart's desire, I envision myself sitting in the cockpit of my Ferrari, having the valet open the doors for my wife and I, and we step out, dressed to impress. I want to experience that type of attention. I feel no shame or hesitation in putting that in here. It may seem shallow to some, but I can't care about that; otherwise, I'd let them write out my goals. I share this with you to, hopefully, give you full liberty to dream your genuine desires and then set them as goals. Life will give you what you ask of it if you ask from the depths of your being.

It's okay to envision yourself as rich in twelve months, three years, and incredibly wealthy in five years. It's okay to fight for a better financial situation and a better future. In order to do so it is imperative that you eliminate some current habits and start enacting the business principles I've carefully laid out for you. Be selfish and ensure your success. I know this: to help anyone, you need to be in a position to help. You can't help the poor if you're one of them.

Did you do it? Did you close your eyes and envision a better you, a better life? Did you write it down? If not, take the time to do that now.

We're almost done; the book will be here when you're done. Give yourself permission to be wildly successful. Don't worry about how things will happen; dream big and turn those dreams into goals by writing them down. Go ahead, do that now...

THE FREEDOM ACHIEVER ACADEMY

I've created The Freedom Achiever Academy for people serious about going after their desired life. People have told me, "I saw you speak years ago and you changed my life." I have to admit, that's a fantastic feeling. However, as the great Zig Ziglar used to say, watching me on stage and implementing what I say is powerful. However, if you want a truly transformative experience, you need to hear the message repeatedly," which is why he made cassette tapes.

Many more people's lives were transformed when they were able to play those tapes over and over.

In the same way, watching me on stage will empower and enlighten you, reading this book will go a little deeper, but if you want the deepest, most-ground-breaking experience with me – send me a Direct Message (D.M.) on my Instagram and find out what my The Freedom Achiever Academy is all about. It could be a life-changer for you, your family, your business, your community, and any cause you are passionate about.

Feel free to reach me on Instagram: David Adam Kurz (@David-AdamKurz)

Or, check out The Freedom Academy here: www.FreedomAchieverAcademy.com

There are self-love rewards in taking action. As you may guess, I'm an action-taker. Come on, U.S. Marine, entrepreneur, speaker, coach, married to a strong, intelligent Latina – I'm like Action Jackson (for those who are much younger than me, that's an 80s movie title) I'm always up to something, whether it's getting up early to hit the gym, selling property, building teams, coaching, being the best husband and father I can be, going to masterminds, or, as is the case this very moment as I write this, being flown to Michigan to speak to a room full of entrepreneurs.

However, there are quiet times when I can inhale deeply, exhale slowly, and enjoy the moment. Often, I'm in my backyard, holding a scotch in my left hand and a cigar in the other, looking at my elegant house from the backyard, seeing my beautiful wife get in her Zen state as she tends to the plants she loves, seeing and hearing the kids and their friends jumping, giggling, and splashing in the pool while the dogs come near me and, after walking around me a couple of times, flop comfortably to nap near me.

The stats say a half-Puerto Rican, half-Jewish kid raised by a single mother for many years in a project in The Bronx should not have this lifestyle, let alone in ritzy Miami.

Then I puff my cigar and say softly, "F*ck the stats. I worked hard for this."

By the time it's time for bed, I am already anticipating the next day when I get to do what it takes to make even more of my dreams come to life.

So, dear reader, what are you going to do tomorrow? Hopefully, not the same things that have gotten you to where you are when you should be so much further ahead. I urge you to take new and more powerful actions. The Freedom Achiever Academy is a resource you should strongly consider. Let us help you brainstorm a plan that will allow you to sometimes inch and sometimes fly you closer to your dream life.

We also created a complete deep dive training on this very book. Because you purchased this book, I want to offer you a $200 discount on this specialized training. Head over to www.TruthAboutFailure.com and sign up for the training. Use the following code to unlock your $200 discount: TRUTH - More information can be found in the resource page of this book.

IN CLOSING

Yes, I quit high school. Yes, I have made many mistakes. But also, yes, I've taken massive action. I went to the Marine Corps and earned a bachelor's degree - Cum Laude, and then I earned my Master's in International business. Yes, I built a multi-million dollar-a-year business – more than once. And yes, I'm not done yet. I'm just getting started. What are you saying yes to?

Oh, and one more thing – you can succeed without failing forward. Goal set, find a mentor, implement new tactics, and take action. Remove failure from your vocabulary. You do not quit!

Screw failure.

ACKNOWLEDGMENTS

First and foremost, my thanks always go to the creator. My faith has found its highs and lows in my lifetime. I have questioned why so many things happen. I have even joked about the quote, "God only gives you what you can handle," with "Sheesh, I wish he didn't trust me to handle so much." :) My faith keeps my heart strong. It keeps my family tight. It guides me daily. And I am so grateful for all the ups and downs because that has molded me into who I am today. And I pray for further guidance and molding to make me a better version of myself each and every day.

My wife, Jennyffer. An incredible wife, mother, thinker, innovator, designer, planner, and so much more. I looked at my wife in 2020 and asked if she would be open to going on a longer motorcycle ride (we both ride Harleys). She asked, "Where?". To which I crazily replied, "Loop around the United States." Her response? In the calmest, most no worried voice in the world, "Sure." Six weeks, 7,000 miles, and 22 states later - we celebrated being home again. That is just a small sample of who my wife is and how much she supports my crazy. She is not only a sideline supporter. She is a, in the jet ready to take over, side-by-side supporter. And I could never ask for a better partner in my life. I am a big thinker and a dreamer. She is very grounded but has no problem riding the most curvy roads with me. I love you for being you, Baby Girl.

Olivia, Amber, Ellie, and Allie. My four ladies. My angels. My daughters. You bring happiness and smiles to my face every day. You encourage me to be better. You entertain me with your jokes and laughter daily.

There is no moment in my life where I do not think about you and if what I am doing will create a legacy you would be proud of.

Mom. My #1 fan. My feisty little Puerto Rican lady. You have supported me my entire life. You fought to be a great mother even with the limited resources and the hours you had to put in with 2 or 3 jobs. It is unbelievable how you had to work so hard, having multiple degrees in education, to raise my brother and me. And even now, in retirement, you are never afraid to invest in me. You are a believer and I will always love you for who you are in my life. I only pray that you are around to see the results of what we did!

Dad. Thank you for cheering me on. Using your decades of success and experience to plug in on what I do and how I do it. Thank you for keeping me connected to my roots with your stories and keeping me grounded in faith. The time we have had is the time we have and I am glad we made the most of it.

Bedros Keuilian. I actually do not personally know Bedros. But I do follow him and listen to his podcasts. I found his YouTube channel on probably one of the lowest moments I have ever had emotionally. It was a crazy moment when it felt like all the world's problems were on my shoulders. When you are working hard to spread a message, you never know who you will affect and how it can change the trajectory of their lives forever. Bedros may have saved my life that day.

Rudy Hernandez. Rudy is the founder of Nu World Title. When I met him, I already had a solid relationship with a title company and was not looking for a change. After meeting him, I knew immediately he was someone I wanted to work with. Fast forward almost a decade and Rudy is a partner and a friend. Never says no to my moments of insanity and always has been there through the highs and lows. He has encouraged me to "do more" each and every day. He has no problem digging into my ideas and processes and calling it how it is. He is the epitome of who you want in your circle. The only problem... he cannot be duplicated. People like him are hard to find. I look forward to the growth we both strive for daily. Nonstop.

Jeannie Echevarría and Jenn Gomez. AKA The Generals. You've been a core piece of my last few moves and I couldn't be prouder to work with you both. My friends. My business partners. Your trust and passion for what we are building together is very appreciated. Thank you.

Robert Palmer. One meeting with you changed the trajectory of my development as a human and entrepreneur. You may not know this but there was a light in me that was very dim. I began to accept my reality. You helped pour gasoline on that fire and created something out of control. My vision got bigger. My dreams look unattainable to others. Thank you for sparking that in me. Let's do big things.

Jean Mones. My brother-in-law and the ride or die. Brother, thank you for more than five years of you, your creativity, your loyalty, and love. You believe in what we are building. And I will forever be grateful to you.

Eli Gonzalez. Thanks for working with me throughout the last few years to help me with this book.

To my teams and employees - no great business is built on the back of one person. It takes many people at many different levels with one dream, one belief, and one mission. Thank you for allowing me to create through you. Thank you for staying on the mission for the big dream, big thinking, and outlandish goals.

RECOMMENDED READING

The Hero Code
By Admiral William H McRaven
We spoke about this book often and I believe the writings and stories in this book will give you tremendous insight on living your best life.

$100M LEADS
By Alex Hormozi
As we said, LEADS are key for any business. This book will guide you through getting some of the best methods in place to lead generate.

INFLUENCE, The Psychology of Persuasion
By Robert B. Cialdini, PH.D
Master influencing people and conversations.

Your Next Five Moves, Master the Art of Business Strategy
Patrick Bet-David
I personally loved this book and read it at a time that made real sense for my business. I recommend it often to leaders building a business.

Amplify Your Influence

By Rene Rodriguez
Becoming an influencer in your business has never been more important. This book will guide you.

The Five Dysfunctions of a Team
By Patrick Lencioni
Every team has its methods and systems. But there are some common dysfunctions that destroy team business. This book helps you avoid them.

The 48 Laws of Power
By Robert Greene
This one is special. It's an incredible book with massive guidance. My advice, read one power a week and practice it best you can.

Relentless
By Tim Grover, Shari Wenk

The Secret of Closing the Sale
By Zig Ziglar, Tom Ziglar

Outwitting the Devil
By Napoleon Hill

RESOURCE PAGE

I've put together a resource page for you in order to give you more information and opportunities in your business.

Below you will find links to resources I want you to take advantage of as an entrepreneur!

Freedom Achiever Academy
FreedomAchieverAcademy.com

The Freedom Achiever Academy is an online training and coaching platform that I have created to help you and your business grow. It's an incredible resource with over 400 training videos, downloadable resources and Q&A's to test your knowledge. Sign up for it and USE IT.

The Freedom Organization
TheFreedomOrganization.com

Learn more about the Freedom Organization, a coaching and consulting company. Inquire about one on one coaching, group coaching, events and more.

Everything you need to connect with David Adam Kurz
EverythingDavidKurz.com

Live link to everything I have, everything I am doing and more!

Truth About Failure Training
TruthAboutFailureBook.com

I designed a full training around this book. I want you to enjoy this book and then do a deep dive on the training. Now, this training is marketed at $495 however; since you have purchased this book, use the code TRUTH and get $200 off today! Better yet, if you purchase 10 books and send us the receipt - we will give you access to this training for FREE.

So, if you want this training for FREE, do the following:

1. Go back to Amazon and purchase 10 books.
2. Take a screenshot of the receipt.
3. Send that screenshot to books@davidadamkurz.com
4. Shortly thereafter you will receive an email with instructions to log into the training.
5. Give these 10 books away to your friends and family.

The Hero Code: Lessons Learned from Lives Well Lived
By William H. McRaven

I don't have a link for this but you can go to Amazon and pick this up. Highly recommended and you will understand the chapter in this book that discusses this book better.

Take Action by David Adam Kurz
DownloadTakeAction.com

You can download this book for $2.99 from this site! And get The Blueprint for FREE. No better way to get your PDF digital copy. If you are a book person like me, you can grab these on Amazon.

Real Estate CE courses
FreedomCEShop.com

If you are looking to become a real estate agent in the United States or want to renew your license, this link will help you in all 50 states. Stay up to date with your CE courses through the Freedom Organizations alliance with the CE Shop.

Solar panel sales outlet
SolarWithFreedom.com

Remember that guy I mentioned in the book that told me about Time Valuement? The one that sold his company for millions of dollars. Well, he launched this amazing solar company nationally and you can sign up for free to become a distributor and earn commissions. This is great for anyone in the real estate industry. Become the conduit for everything your homeowners need and make some cash flow while you do it.

Take your DISC Profile Test

FreedomDISCTest.com

I am Abelson DISC Certified. Dr. Michael Abelson has partnered with me to offer you the personality test FREE.

Take your DISC Profile test here and learn more about you, your methods and why you do things the way you do. It's an excellent way to learn how to focus on the things you can excel at quickly.

www.ingramcontent.com/pod-product-compliance
Lightning Source LLC
Chambersburg PA
CBHW060535130626
46553CB00002B/761